Be My Son

Be My Son

J. ROY LEGERE

Ave Maria Press / Notre Dame / Indiana 46556

Nihil Obstat: Reverend Charles Fidler, O.C.S.O.

Imprimatur: †Vincent J. Hines, D.D., J.C.D.
        Bishop of Norwich

The Nihil Obstat and Imprimatur are official declarations that a book or pamphlet is free of doctrinal or moral error. No implication is contained therein that those who have granted the Nihil Obstat and Imprimatur agree with the contents, opinions or statements expressed.

Library of Congress Catalog Card Number: 76-41592

International Standard Book Number: 0-87793-120-8 (Cloth)
                                    0-87793-121-6 (Paper)

Art by Tom Hojnacki

Cover photo by H. Armstrong Roberts

Printed in the United States of America

To fall in love with God
    is the greatest of all romances;
To seek him, the greatest adventure;
To find him, the greatest human achievement.

—Saint Augustine

The author wishes to thank, warmly and prayerfully, all who have helped in the writing of this book, as well as all who, under God, have helped in the making of his life story.

Contents

Introduction

Be My Son is the record of one man's genuine response to a divine call, a response of simplicity and love.

As you read this book, you will see God's love unfolding in the life of someone who felt abandoned, alone and helpless, someone the world at large considered worthless. You may find it surprising that God would intervene so dramatically in our day, as he did with Roy Legere; but God's ways are not necessarily ours. Throughout history, God has shown himself to be master of his own riches. His approaches are not determined by one's slot in human history, social status, or concept of how he *should* act. Pope Paul VI has stressed repeatedly that simple faith is the key to all God's dealings with men. Finding a man of simple faith, God chose him and formed him according to his own designs.

St. John's Gospel brings home the consoling fact that Christ enlightens every man who comes into the world; this light can then be a source of light to others. This is, in fact, the central message of Vatican II to the laity: each individual layman must be a God-bearer, a witness to the fact that God lives.

The Council brought to light many new stresses concerning the dignity and mission of the laity. An example is the call to holiness addressed to all men in *Lumen Gentium*, a reminder that all without exception are called to sanctity. The title of the *Decree on the Apostolate of the Laity* speaks for itself; there is much for every

9

layman to do on behalf of God's kingdom. Certainly, this book antedates Vatican II; yet the author's life embodies the Council's message. Christ personally taught him to live the eternal truths expressed in the Council long before Vatican II was ever dreamed of.

Each man is unique; no one exactly copies another's path to God within the People of God. Christ is concerned with each one's degree of response and commitment in the circumstances surrounding him. The same Christ extends his love today to those living in poverty and rejection, as well as in plenty. However complex society has become, his call is still substantially, eternally the same: "My son, give me your heart." Men's lives may change in appearances, but the substance of the Christ-life, the life of man with God, is changeless: faith, hope and love.

Be My Son stands as a beacon of hope to all those who feel that the obstacles separating them from God are insurmountable. As a result of his formation by Christ, the author has been active full time since 1968 on behalf of the Christ he knows and loves so well. The sufferings, trials and temptations continue, but love has taught perseverance. The message of his apostolate is simply scripture, the Council documents, the teachings of the Church and Christ's Vicar. His apostolate answers the crying need of many men and women for eternal truth — expressing it in today's language, restating what Jesus Christ personally taught him from his youth.

The author's story is a fulfillment of the call of the Council Fathers: "Each individual layman must stand before the world as a witness to the resurrection and life of the Lord Jesus and as a sign that God lives . . . in a word, 'what the soul is to the body, let Christians be to the world' " *(Lumen Gentium,* IV, 38).

—Donald J. Philip

1. Without Benefit of Marriage

It was a late October afternoon, a discouraging and miserable day for me, a 20-year-old man, bedridden with rheumatic fever and inflammatory rheumatism. I was lying on a cot in a corner of a room dimly lit by a kerosene lamp. I wasn't too warm, for my family's five-room slum house was heated only by a small kitchen oil stove. The dirt cellar, half filled with water, added to the damp climate of the room. I had been sick since July, and had made little progress; I wasn't getting proper diet or sufficient medical care. Even worse, my spiritual state was no comfort at all. I had seldom attended church services in the previous three years; though I still believed in God, I thought him cold, impersonal and severe. I regarded my long illness, in fact, as a direct punishment from him.

In childhood, I had had a vague notion of Christ. I learned a little about him from the Sisters at school and looked up to him as a remarkable historical person. I believed he was God's Son, and there were times I envied the people who knew him, heard his words, felt his power. I knew some fundamental Christian doctrine, but this seemed to be only a list of negatives: "Don't do this; don't do that!" The Christian way of life seemed meant for the strong, not for someone like me. For the eight years preceding my illness I had been caught up in a segment of society anything but conducive to virtuous living, and had succumbed to the temptations of my wretched surroundings.

13

Resting on my pillow, hands tucked under my head, I was feeling very sorry for myself. Nobody really cared for me. My friends rarely visited me, and the rest of my family, needing a change of pace from having spent so much time caring for me, sometimes left me alone for hours at a stretch. I needed great care, for I was completely helpless.

At this moment, when my feeling of desolation was at an all-time low and I was drowning in waves of self-pity, my whole attitude toward life, and especially toward God, was instantly changed by recalling my first meeting with Jesus Christ. The eternal Son of God flooded my mind with the light of his grace, with flashes of insight that unveiled for me the realities of a world far beyond my past experience. Recalling this mysterious meeting and the many that followed brought me to my senses, and I found the strength to continue my struggle for life. He made me understand truths that lay far beyond the reach of my senses. He totally transformed my thinking, enabling me to rebuild the structure of my life out of its many tattered fragments.

The beginnings of my life were indeed fragmented. My birth caused an upheaval in family relations that lasted for years. My mother, Sylvia Legere, already had three children: Beatrice, 12; Fidele, ten; and Raymond, an infant of two. I was born on February 17, 1922, in Randolph, a suburb of St. John, New Brunswick, Canada. The house that became my home at birth was a tenement shared by some relatives who had taken my family in. My widowed mother had for many months been the target of merciless abuse because she was about to give birth to a child without the benefit of marriage. She was 32 years old.

Only two parties were really interested in me or wanted me: my mother, naturally; and the Church, ever aware of the dignity of any human being. My mother resisted every effort on the part of relatives to make her give me away. She decided to keep me with her and raise me to the best of her ability, come what may. Within a few days she had me baptized Joseph Roy, thereby making it possible for the baby that only she wanted to become an adopted son of God the Father. I was taken to the Church of St. Rose of Lima in Fairville, which served the people of Randolph.

When I was a year old, my family moved to Port Elgin, where my mother had lived before my birth. Its chief industries were smelt fishing, Hickman's Lumber Mill and McGee's Canning Factory. Many of the townspeople were employed in lumber and lobster camps in surrounding areas. Port Elgin had one hotel, three general stores, a drugstore, and two churches, one Protestant and one Catholic. A river divided the town into two sections, connected by two covered wooden bridges. Resting on the shores of the Bay of Fundy, it is most scenic in the summer, but bitterly cold in the winter. We lived on Green Road, a dirt path leading to the tiny railroad station at the water's edge. Near our home was a huge drawbridge and a wharf used by many large boats which carried supplies for the industries in town. Most of the townsfolk were descendants of the many French families who had settled there during the dispersion of the Acadians.

Soon after our arrival, my mother met Paul Richard, a local butcher. He was a widower with grown children and 26 years her senior. In due time, he asked her to marry him. They decided to emigrate to the United States to get away from the bitterness that arose among their relatives when they heard of the impending May-September marriage. He preceded her to Hazardville, a suburb of Enfield, Connecticut, where he found work, then rented and furnished a tenement for us. By selling our meager possessions, we were able to pay for our long journey to the United States.

We arrived in Hazardville in mid-June, 1923. My mother and Paul Richard were married in St. Patrick's Church in Thompsonville. Some of Papa Richard's children who lived in the area resented my mother, who had a lonely time of it for the first three years of her stay in Hazardville. However, each of them came around to visit after a time, and relations became friendly. Two of her stepchildren lived nearby and gave Mama encouragement whenever her spirits were low. Papa took her to card parties and she soon made several good friends. She learned to speak English fluently. Beatrice and Fidele were enrolled in school under their own family name. Our family had blended into community life.

I don't remember much of Papa until I reached the age of six, but I am told that he showed me much love and affection in my formative years. I can recall kneeling at his side as he taught me to pray.

In the next two years, two children, Sylvester and Mary Mae, were born into our family. In 1928, we moved to Thompsonville to be closer to the Bigelow-Sanford Carpet Mill where my mother and father both worked. Beatrice left school to look after the three smaller children. In the evening, the three of us would perch on Papa's lap and chair for bedtime stories and night prayers. He never read from a book; instead he created the stories as he went along. We spent many delightful evenings with this gentle man.

Papa loved to walk. I can remember him taking us for walks along the banks of the Connecticut River, explaining the world around us and doling out our favorite candy — orange gumdrops. The world was big and scary to me then. However, when the river, bridges, trucks and roaring trains would frighten me, the firm grip of Papa's hand on mine brought peace and a sense of security. In his company, I felt that nothing could ever harm me. His arms were big and strong. So was his swift hand — as I found out whenever I needed correcting.

Before long, however, the security that my mother's remarriage had afforded me was shattered. One day, some of us were playing a game in which we called out our full name. I said that mine was Roy Richard. In a sarcastic tone of voice, a woman standing nearby commented: "Your name is *not* Roy Richard. Paul Richard is not your father." This disturbed me greatly; and that night when Mama was getting me ready for bed I asked her if Papa was my real father. She answered tactfully, "Roy, your own father died when you were very small. Papa is really your stepfather." I was satisfied with this explanation. My love for Papa didn't diminish. I did, however, secretly wonder if he loved me as much as the others, though I never observed any distinction between his affection for me and for his own flesh and blood. He used to hear my catechism in preparation for First Holy Communion. I remember running home from school to show him the stars I had received for knowing my lessons and he seemed especially proud of my ability to learn things about our Faith. He and my mother appreciated the goodness of the Sisters in taking such an active interest in my training. They showed me great love and affection.

In the fall of 1928, Papa's health began to deteriorate. He began to take radium treatments for a growth on the side of his face. By early 1929, he was bedridden. On Saturday, April 18, Mother asked him if he wanted her to stay at home with him. He replied, "If I need you, I will send for you. You can go to work." Shortly before noon, he called me to his side and asked me to run down to the mill gate at Bigelow-Sanford's and leave a message for my mother to come home. I ran as fast as my legs would carry me. Breathless, I told the guard at the gate to send Mother home; Papa was very sick. She must have expected the worst, for she brought Fidele and Beatrice with her. I read trouble in their faces as they entered the house. I remember Mother coming into Papa's bedroom and speaking some reassuring words to him.

It was a weekend of chaotic activity and deep sorrow. I heard

Mama send Fidele for a priest and ask Beatrice to call the visiting nurse. I went in to see Papa, stood by his bed and asked him how he felt. He just looked at me and quietly smiled. Soon the priest came to anoint him. I helped Mama set up the candles and crucifix next to his bed. I remember sitting near the stairway facing the bedroom, watching all that was going on. Fear came into my heart as I saw Mama and Beatrice crying. As the priest was leaving, he spoke to me, but I can't recall what he said. Soon after the priest left, the visiting nurse arrived and helped make Papa comfortable. She told us that she thought death would come that day. It was hard for me to believe, for Papa and Mama were talking quietly together for a long time. Later, Mama told me how sorry he was that he wouldn't be able to see me make my First Holy Communion in May. He called my brother Fidele to his bedside and the last words I heard him say were, "Take good care of the kids." Shortly after noon he slipped into a coma. At two o'clock, we knelt reciting the sorrowful mysteries of the rosary as God called Papa home.

I was very much afraid of death, so I knelt as close to the door as possible without going out of the room. When death claimed her beloved husband, my mother's quiet sobbing broke into hysterical screams. They led her past me as I stared in horror at the dark power of death. I don't know how to describe the misery and sorrow that I felt; I only knew that I would miss this gentle man. We had loved and trusted each other. I watched someone pull the sheet over his face, then I left the room with an empty heart. I watched relatives and friends come and go, not fully realizing the impact the passing of this man would have on our family. On the morning of the funeral, my big brother Fidele lifted me up over the casket that I might get a last look at Papa, and I kissed him on the forehead. As I look back to those early years, knowing what I now see in Jesus Christ, I can see his love, affection and tenderness for little children so clearly reflected in this wonderful man I will always remember as Papa Richard.

For a long time after Papa's death, my mother cried softly as she sat in the early shadows of the evening. Her troubles were compounded by the stock market crash in 1929, whose effect was felt in working conditions throughout the country. Mama kept a housekeeper to look after us so that she, Beatrice and Fidele could earn enough to keep our family together. Soon their working hours were cut, and in order to make ends meet, Mama took in two boarders. This didn't help enough, and soon we began moving from one home to another, each smaller and poorer than the one before. In a short time we were reduced to living in four rooms at 19 Martin Street, in the north end of Thompsonville. All around us people were being laid off, bread lines were forming, and the welfare offices were filled by those suffering from the misery of the Depression. Often, we were saved from complete destitution by food baskets and other help from local merchants, the Elks Club, the St. John the Baptist Society, and other clubs in our town. Many times I took home bundles of clothing that had been gathered for us by the Sisters at school. I have many memories of the kindness of these nuns, and my school friends.

In the years following Papa's death, Mother received a continual flow of letters from her family in Canada, urging her to come back home, assuring her that we would all be better off with them. When working hours in Connecticut dwindled, Mom decided to listen to her relatives' advice, and began packing clothes and selling furniture. We children had heard so much about Canada and its country life that our excitement built up to a high pitch. We hardly slept nights as June 2 drew near. On the afternoon of that fateful day, we boarded a train and headed for what was to turn out to be a shattering of all our dreams.

2. Destination Heartbreak

After a long and exciting train ride back to Canada, we were met at the Port Elgin station by four of our cousins: Laura, Doris, Leona and William Bourque. They were the children of Uncle Morris and Aunt Minnie (the sister of my mother's first husband). They welcomed us excitedly and led us across the drawbridge, helping us with our baggage. Aunt Minnie came running down the track to meet us, crying as she hugged and kissed us all in turn. Many relatives came out of their houses to greet us as we made our way toward Uncle Morris' home, which was situated on a high bank with its back door facing the tracks. Grandma Legere, who lived with them, came slowly to meet us as we neared the house. After she made the rounds, she came over to me and put her hands on my shoulders. Her face wet with tears, she looked into my eyes and said, "So this is Roy." I got a good warm hug from the little old lady I thought was my grandmother.

That evening, Aunt Minnie's house was filled with relatives and friends who came to renew old acquaintances. I watched with great excitement and anticipation, hoping that at last we would be able to live where I could see my mother smile more often. I missed Fidele, for he and Mary (whom he had met in Thompsonville) were now married, and had taken another train to Memramcook to settle near some other relatives.

After a few days' rest, Mom and Beatrice began looking for jobs. Day after day for over three weeks they would leave home hopefully in the morning, then return tired and discouraged at night. Someone suggested that my mother visit the parish priest and ask his advice. He told her it might be best to place the four children, at least temporarily, in a Catholic orphanage not too far from Port Elgin. He felt this would give her and Beatrice a chance to branch out farther away from town and perhaps find satisfactory jobs. Then they could save enough to establish us later on in a home of our own. The next morning my mother wrote to the orphanage, explaining our situation. In a few days she received a reply telling her that we would be very welcome at St. Joseph's Home, a combination old-age home and orphanage, run by the Sisters of Charity, a French-Canadian order whose motherhouse was in the Province of Quebec.

One night after getting us all ready for bed, my mother called us into the parlor where she was sitting with Uncle Morris, Beatrice, Aunt Minnie and Grandma. They explained to us why they were placing us in the orphanage for a time. None of us liked the idea, to say the least. Aunt Minnie broke into the painful conversation: "Sylvia, I would be very happy to have Roy live with us until you can find a home of your own. My sister Maggie said that she would be willing to take Raymond." That would leave Sylvester and Mae to go to the orphanage alone, an idea that bothered my mother very much. She objected, "I don't want to see them separated. It is bad enough that they have to live away from me, and if one or two have to go to the home, it is only right that they should all go together." So it was decided. A few days later, the pastor came with his car and off we went to the orphanage.

Strangely enough, though I was considered the most emotional of the four, I did not cry when mother turned us over to the Sisters at the home, but it was one of the darkest hours of my life. I saw my little sister Mae being led away by a bigger girl to the section of the orphanage assigned for girls. One of the boys came to take the three of us to the dormitory, where single beds were lined up like those in an army camp. I had been taught a little about the spirit of sacrifice, and I readily adapted myself to the regimented routine of a drab and uninviting orphanage existence. Raymond and Sylvester were a source of sadness and discomfort — Raymond cried at the drop of a hat, and Syl was stubborn toward the nuns. He kept telling me to try to correct the Sisters. The nuns spoke in broken English, and I understood French a little; that was why I became the "middle man" on my brother's behalf.

I, too, was unhappy with the Sisters. They were strict and poker-faced. They ran the orphanage in a manner that made religion quite odious to us. It was a very sharp contrast to the Christ-like way of living I had learned from the Sisters in Enfield, who had always encouraged me to practice my faith in a spirit of joy and cheerfulness rather than of servile fear. Yet, the Sisters at the orphanage did teach me to spend my time wisely. I learned to iron clothes, make beds, wait on tables and many other chores that would come in handy years later. It was a good thing that I was kept very busy; otherwise I would not have overcome the terrible feeling that I had. It was as if I had been deserted by my mother. Many weeks passed before I knew where she was or what she was doing. My only ray of comfort was the presence of Jesus in the Blessed Sacrament in the chapel. If it hadn't been for my frequent Communions, that orphanage would have been a "hell on earth" for me. There was much hatred and resentment among the children toward the nuns. I have often wondered how many orphans kept their faith after leaving their supervision. The atmosphere in that home made us feel that Christianity could sadden our hearts rather than give us liberty of spirit — which it promised us as children of God.

Every morning when the priest would raise the Host during Mass, my brothers and I would whisper, "Jesus, get us out of here!" We urged each other to pester Christ in this way until he did get us out.

My sister Mae was the first to leave. One day, a nun came over to me and told me that my mother's sister, Zoey, had taken Mae to live with her in St. John. Not long after, my brothers and I were called to the parlor dressed in our black shirts and trousers. (My brother Syl used to say they made us look like "Mussolini's Black Shirts!") How happy I was to see Fidele and his wife Mary waiting to take us home. Mom and Beatrice had sent them money, asking them to find a place where we could live. Mom was working for some rich people somewhere in Nova Scotia.

We lived for several weeks with one of Mary's sisters in a place called Legere's Corner. Then we moved with Mary and Fidele to Humphrey, New Brunswick, where we sublet a tenement for part of the winter. While we lived there, we were exposed to immoral conduct by some unmarried persons living in the same house. This was the beginning of a long descent toward moral and religious disintegration occasioned by the poverty which forced us to live with many unfortunate types of people as we moved like gypsies from one town to another.

In February, we moved to an apartment in Lewisville, New Brunswick, and during the spring and summer there I learned to read and speak French very well. We went to Mass every Sunday, and after Mass recited the rosary with Mary and Fidele. Poverty was, increasingly, our lot in life. In one year, Fidele was able to find only one week's work, during which he earned fuel for part of the winter. My mother was able to obtain some welfare help for us and we survived, with the added help of some neighbors. One act of kindness stands out in my memory. On February 17, my 11th birthday, I was plowing my way home from school through very deep snow and, as I passed a neighbor's house, I heard someone call to me. As I drew near, the whole family came to the door, sang "Happy Birthday," and presented me with a beautiful three-layered birthday cake! When I was able to catch my breath, I thanked them from the bottom of my heart. I couldn't remember the last time I'd had a cake for my birthday. I carried that cake home with positive reverence, for it was a symbol of my neighbor's love.

My mother came to visit us later and brought some clothes that we badly needed. We talked of many things; we dreamed and planned what we would do for her when we grew up. One night during Mama's visit, I woke up to the sound of what seemed to be an argument. As I neared the kitchen, I heard my mother crying. She was telling Fidele and Mary that she would never tell anyone my father's name. When they saw me standing in the door, they immediately became silent. They all seemed embarrassed and sent me back to bed. I was very confused, for I thought Fidele knew that my father's name was the same as his. I simply didn't understand, and I fell asleep feeling vaguely sorry for Mom.

In May, we moved again. We piled all our furniture on a large hayrack drawn by two husky horses and moved out to a farming area called Gilbert's Corner. We struggled for a while to pay our rent, and when we fell behind, had to move again. There was a very kind widow who took an interest in me and invited me to spend most of the summer living with her and her grown children. They loved me and took care of me as one of their own. They gave me a bike, a calf of my own, and some ducks to raise. I helped with the farm work; I drove the horses and helped care for the cattle. I even learned to ride horseback! One day one of the boys put me on the bare back of a large horse and threw a pebble at it; the horse raced toward the drinking well with me hanging on to the reins, too stunned to cry out. I never mounted a horse again.

My mother found a job in the mining town of Minto, New

Brunswick. Although my farmer friends urged her to let them adopt me, she firmly refused. She let me stay on with them, though, sending my brothers and sister to other relatives and friends. The kind lady showed me great love and affection, but I still missed my mother a great deal. While living with these wonderful friends, I would often awaken at night crying, having dreamt that I was back home in Connecticut with Mama and Papa Richard, only to find myself in a strange home, a strange bed. This good woman would come to me and hug me, telling me, "Someday you will have a happy home of your own."

Toward the end of August, Mom came and took me to live with her in Moncton, New Brunswick, in a small apartment at the rear of an empty store. For two months we lived in this dreadful place that leaked like a basket whenever it rained. Mom tried to get some welfare aid, but was told that we hadn't been residents of the city long enough to receive it. They suggested that we go to Port Elgin where they felt we would be well received because my mother had lived there for so many years. So we moved again to Port Elgin, living for a time with one of Mom's sisters-in-law, who was expecting her fourth child. One day this woman got angry with me and came at me with a butcher knife saying, "I'll cut your heart out before you go to bed tonight!" We had moved into an environment of new tension.

After several weeks, due to some argument, our family was thrown out into the street. My mother found a deserted shack near the river on Green Road, on the "wrong side of the tracks." The road came to a dead end at the town dump. The shack had only two rooms and a small attic which we reached by ladder. There was no cellar to protect us from the dampness, and no running water. The attic ceiling was too low for beds so we put our mattresses on the floor. We scarcely endured the dampness as the tide sometimes touched the back of our shack.

To offset the misery of our poor existence, we played our phonograph records for square dancing and did our best to keep laughing instead of crying. We missed Sunday Mass more and more often because we were ashamed of our poor clothing, and we picked up the vulgar language of the street. We were slowly slipping into a way of life unknown to us before. We put all our efforts into the struggle for bodily survival. As for our souls, we were too tired and poor to do much about them.

The parish priest visited us once in a while and encouraged us to go to Mass and to pray. He even brought some wood for us and boots for us boys. We went to confession and Communion on occasion, but the things we saw and heard between Sundays had their ill effect, and most of us children were in one degree or another saying and doing things far beyond our years. Socially and morally we were at the very bottom of the barrel. Occasionally, I would get a burst of religious fervor, but it would quickly pass. Sometimes I longed to be a priest, to "go about doing good," but our living conditions smothered such high ideals.

My mother worked as a chambermaid in a hotel, earning $1.75 a week. She often brought home scraps from the hotel kitchen which we youngsters eagerly devoured. It was hard for her to feed a family of four children (for Mae was now living with us again). Water had to be carried long distances when the nearby wells were low. I had to scrub floors, wash clothes and iron. We all pitched in as well as we could to make our existence bearable. Sometimes I helped my mother scrub the railroad station for the three dollars needed to pay our rent.

When we left Connecticut I had been promoted to the sixth grade. But with all the new schools I entered, each with different requirements and standards, I never made any further progress. At the age of 15, I was still in the sixth grade. I was a hopeless case, and had come, I thought, to the end of my formal education.

After a while, we moved to another house. Again it was cold and without running water and toilet facilities, but it was better than the shack. The winters were harsh near the Bay of Fundy. Our molasses froze in the jugs; our water buckets froze solid in the pantry. For fuel, mother had us gather shore wood and dry it out in the sun. Sometimes we bought a cord of long birch and helped her cut it with a saw in the freezing cold by lamplight. Sometimes we had real coal — picked up from freighters — which kept us from freezing in our beds.

The next year we moved in with a widower and his three children. They lived in a large house and wanted to take in boarders. Mom continued working and Beatrice came from Nova Scotia to help run the house. Between the two families and the other boarders, we had a full house. In that home I came into contact with powers virtually of hell. By the time I was 12, I had seen and heard enough to last me a lifetime. My young eyes saw things that one can read about only in those cheap paperback novels which so easily corrupt all who share their contents. I began to long for the peace I had known in the United States, and even that of my unhappy orphanage life. When Mother became aware of our wretched moral situation, she talked to a priest who urged her to go back to the shack on Green Road, to save her children from complete corruption. He arranged for us to get $2.25 a week from the welfare department. The man in charge of issuing welfare handouts made our life miserable. I was always the one to pick up the groceries or whatever we needed at the general store where this man worked. No one but God and I knew what I went through week after week as I went to beg for our family's survival. When I asked the man in charge for the groceries, he would say, "Well, well, here is one of Sylvia's gang!" He treated me and my family with ridicule and contempt.

For me, God seemed very much like a remote character in a fairy tale in the face of so much misery and ugly destitution. I remember lying in bed fully clothed, trying to keep warm, and wondering what God was really like. Could it be that he was a good God, and yet allowed little children to suffer so much pain and hardship? Many times I got down on my knees in our tiny bedroom and prayed to Papa Richard, begging him to tell God to look after us and get us out of this rut somehow. I often thought of the happy days I had spent with him. I used to steal away once in a while to kneel in church, praying to Jesus in the Blessed Sacrament. I told him that I didn't really want to miss Mass on Sundays, but the people had laughed at us so much and so many times that we didn't have the courage anymore to come to church when other people were there.

One day, the parish priest came into church, saw me, and struck up a conversation. He asked me about my hopes for the future and mentioned something about the priesthood. I said, "Yes, I have thought about it once in a while, but I could never see it happening to me." Not many days passed when he came to see my mother to ask if she would let him place me in a boarding school — but only on the condition that the break with my family be complete. Mom spoke to me, and I decided against it. I longed for all the physical and spiritual security this change might afford me; I dreamed of learning a great deal about God as I recalled how I had enjoyed the teachings of faith under the care of the Sisters in Enfield. But I couldn't leave the people with whom I belonged and whom I loved so much.

One day, when I told my mother that I thought I would like to be a priest, she shocked me by saying, "You can't be." No explanation was given, and all my questions would not move her to tell me why. One day I found out. Before leaving for work, she asked me to go upstairs and look in one of the trunks for a pair of curtains for the kitchen, which I was to iron and hang sometime during the day. Later, while rummaging through the trunk, I found a small cardboard box which seemed unusually heavy for its size. Curiosity made me open it and in it I found two casket plates. One was for Richard, and on the other was written the name of my mother's first husband, Edmund Legere. When I read the date of his death, I started to figure out how old I was when he died. I started, "Let's see, I was born in 1922 — he died in 19........!" The moon, the sun and the stars fell on my head. "Oh God, I'm a bastard!" I was kneeling near the trunk, too stunned to move. With all my other miseries, that was all I needed to make me sick and tired of living. As much as I feared death, I wanted somehow to be out of a life that was so full of shame and heartache. Now I knew why my playmates would shriek with laughter whenever they would fight with me: "I know who *my* father is, ha! ha! ha!" Now I knew why I couldn't be a priest.

As I held the casket plate in my hand, I aged many years. I was tempted to hate my mother and "the man." I knew enough about sex to know that there was, somewhere, some man whose blood ran through my veins. I sat for several minutes, then a very new and very deep sword cut into my aching heart, making a terrible wound. I began to feel that perhaps I was the reason why our family was undergoing so much misfortune: we were being punished by God! Before he hadn't seemed to me like the God described by the priests and nuns. I just couldn't picture him as being merciful or understanding or even very wise in allowing his innocent creatures to undergo so much evil and hardship. Now came the nagging thought: were we so innocent?

Many things came back to my mind as I knelt there sitting on my heels, my head bowed in shame and sorrow. I remembered overhearing the discussion between Fidele and Mom. I felt that I didn't belong to the human race anymore. I didn't know much about the rate of these births in the world, so I thought that, in the vast family of man, what had happened to me was a very rare thing. I felt I was destined by God to be nothing, to be looked down upon, and that my future would be one of constant sorrow and shame. The saddest part of all was the thought that, being the fruit of such an event, God would never want any part of me. I remembered the glances from my relatives whenever I walked into their presence, and the discussions that had broken up when I walked in unexpectedly. Now things began to make a little more sense to me as I recalled the questions and comments: "Who do *you* think Roy looks like? . . . He doesn't look like any of the others . . . . He's much fairer . . . . His mannerisms are different." If I had only known then what God is really like, what happened to me in that room could have been softened and its hurtful effects completely avoided. I wanted to run away from everybody. I didn't know how I was even going to look at my mother and the other members of the family when they came home. I felt I could never walk with my head up again. I dreaded going downtown. I just wanted to get away and go someplace where nobody knew me or my background.

At last I knew why the man in the general store snickered, smirked and laughed whenever I went to ask for food. I took to thinking that I would be offending God by my presence in his church, so I didn't mind not going to Mass or into church anymore. I honestly believed that he didn't want the "likes of me" there. Because of the Jansenistic atmosphere in which we lived, I was convinced that my mother and my unknown father, along with myself, could never get to heaven.

I was at that age when young men begin to feel an inner conflict from their rising passions, which they cannot fully understand. I thought that I would never be able to master these passions because of the special circumstances of my birth. But despite all the pain I suffered, I knew my mother loved me very much and had gone through a great deal because of me; and this made me love her all the more. I did, however, make up my mind to try to find my father someday. I closed the lid of the trunk and I also sealed my lips. For many, many years my mother did not know that I knew the secret she had been unable to share with me.

3. A Ray of Hope

In the summer of 1934, my mother decided to go to Moncton to look for a better job. Before she left, she went to see the mayor of Port Elgin. He agreed to give us a weekly welfare allowance while she was away—the princely sum of $4.35. The storekeeper still humiliated me every time I went to buy food with our welfare check. In November, the mayor decided to put the four of us children in an orphanage because Mom had not yet come for us. When he told me his plan, I ran all the way home to tell Beatrice, terrified that our home was to be broken up again.

This news was added to another anxiety. We hadn't heard from Mom for several weeks. We did not know that she was seriously ill from a gallbladder attack. She had had many minor spasms over the years, but now she was in severe distress. Beatrice sent an urgent note telling Mom of our new trouble. In a few days, Mother walked in unexpectedly, leaving her sickbed to try to keep her family together. My joy at her coming faded away as I saw her thin face; she looked more dead than alive. I felt sure I would soon lose her. She sent for the Royal Canadian Mounted Police, and told them of the mayor's plan. The constable told her that since Syl and Mae were American citizens, they couldn't be placed anywhere against her wishes, and added that it would cost the mayor more to board Raymond and me that he was giving us for our whole family. He went with Mother to see the mayor, and the plan was dropped.

Mother decided to take us back to Moncton with her. An acquaintance of hers, Theophile Melanson, had asked her to marry him, and although she wasn't in love with him, she was fond of him and respected him. So she had agreed to marry this widower who was almost as poor as we. He met us at the station and took us by taxi to the six-room flat he was renting. With two front rooms rented to another party, we had the four back rooms, two of them without windows. As soon as we arrived, Mom had to be put to bed. She grew worse in spite of Beatrice's loving care.

Mr. Melanson had a small war pension that helped to pay the rent and buy food. Our meals consisted of pancakes, bread, potatoes, turnips and molasses. We all drank black tea; milk was a very rare treat for us children. Mr. Melanson had permission to go to the Canadian Railway Depot, where discarded boxcars were sent in, and break these up for firewood. We spent many cold hours breaking boards off and pulling them home on a sled the three miles to our house. We had only a kitchen stove to keep the house warm. On very cold days we took turns putting our feet in the oven.

On the doctor's advice, my mother wrote to the mayor of Port Elgin, asking for a paper that would admit her to the hospital for a major operation. Several weeks passed, during which I saw Mother suffer indescribable agony. She couldn't even keep water on her stomach. I had seen grape juice advertised in a store window as a remedy for weak stomachs. I sold newspapers for three days in order to buy a bottle of this juice which I felt would surely help her get well. The day I bought it, I ran all the way home, very excited, sure that once my mother had tasted this magic potion she would be cured. I was disconsolate a day later when she was no better.

One day, two nuns who had heard of her illness came to visit Mom. They gave us some medals and talked to us about God. I thoroughly enjoyed their company. After they left, Mom called me to her bedside and asked me to have the family begin a novena to the Sacred Heart, praying that the mayor of Port Elgin would pay for her to enter the hospital. We had a statue of the Sacred Heart which I placed near Mom's bed. I made a little altar, and sold newspapers to buy candles and paper flowers for this simple shrine. Every night we gathered around her bed to pray. We prayed for many things: for heat, health, money, food, clothing. We had become destitute; I was sent to secondhand shops to sell some religious pictures and statues we all loved, my mother's wedding rings, and some fineries long preserved in her trunk. I set out on many begging expeditions. Someone gave me a nice collie puppy, which I had to sell for 75 cents to buy bread and molasses. On cold winter mornings, Mr. Melanson awakened us to sell papers on street corners. Sometimes good-hearted people called me up to their apartments for a hot drink; others gave me generous tips, as well as cakes and sandwiches.

The days came and went, with no word from the mayor. Christmas came, the loneliest Christmas of my life. When we returned from Mass on Christmas Day, the Canadian Legion brought us each a gift and a bag of candy. Beatrice and I had put up a tree in the bedroom, where I spent part of Christmas afternoon crying. I thought Mom would die soon, and I found myself longing to see the man who was my father. (I often wondered if he ever thought of me or cared how I was making out in life.) That afternoon, I took Syl and Mae to the Salvation Army Citadel for Christmas dinner and presents from Santa Claus. Although the officer knew we were Catholics, he put his arm around my shoulder and led us to the well-stocked table. We ate our fill for the first time in many months. I wished that Mom and the rest of the family could have been there with us. As we left, the officer gave me a warm overcoat.

A few days later, I was shocked when a priest stormed into our tenement and began shouting at Mother. Someone had told him that she and Mr. Melanson were putting off their marriage and scandalizing us children. I stood there horrified as he pronounced maledictions on our house and family. I ran to my room and prayed to Jesus not to abandon us. That night as we knelt around the statue of the Sacred Heart, the feeling overcame me that Jesus didn't care what happened to us because I was the "fruit of sin," as I had heard someone say. I felt that he was done with our family and we would all end up in hell. As my lips uttered the prayers, my heart welled up, and from it poured all the anguish and aching loneliness of a soul abandoned to the heart of God. When we said the words, "Jesus, help of the poor," I put my head on the table at the foot of the statue and cried for several minutes. The family stopped praying to cry with me.

A few days later as I turned a corner, I ran headlong into the mayor of Port Elgin. He said, "Hi, I've been looking for you people." He told me he had come to sign the papers for my mother to be operated on. He asked how she was, and I told him all about our troubles. It was the first and last time he showed me any kindness. Mom underwent surgery a short time later; we waited at home, praying. A few days later, I found Mr. Melanson crying in the woodshed. When I asked what was wrong, he told me the doctor had given up hope for Mom. Beatrice took us boys to church, and we knelt before the Blessed Sacrament for a long time, begging him to let our mother live. The next day we were told she would recover. Several days after her discharge from the hospital, my mother and Mr. Melanson were married in Assumption Rectory. When they returned home, some friends of Mr. Melanson brought a cake and some food, and we had a poor man's celebration. We sang French-Canadian songs, much happier than we had been for a long time. I slept better that night, with high hopes that now Jesus and our family would become better friends.

As the Depression got worse, we settled into the rut of poverty. I was often sent to beg for broken cookies and cakes at a large cookie factory near our home. I kept hoping that each begging tour would be my last, or at least that I would overcome the shame and timidity I experienced every time I approached someone for food or clothing. The children in our new neighborhood knew of my begging expeditions, and I suffered much from their cruel taunts. I was the object of their contempt because we did not attend Mass regularly or observe the season of Lent.

When my folks announced that we were moving to a new house at Newton Heights, another district of Moncton, I had mixed emotions. I was happy to leave the scorn and hate of these children, but dreaded another gypsy moving spree. One day, just before we moved, I was stopped on the street by a strange man. He asked my name and address and arranged to meet my mother. I'd had my first encounter with a truant officer. He made Mom register us for school and ordered us to attend classes at once. With Sylvester and Mae, I was sent to St. Bernard's School. The Board of Education insisted that I be registered under my mother's former name, so for the first time in my life I used the name, Roy Legere. I enjoyed the atmosphere of this parochial school; it was joyful, warm and friendly. We walked three miles to school, passing through some marshlands on the way from our new home, which was on top of a steep hill. The countryside was open, damp and cold.

We had moved into the top floor of a six-room house, which we shared with my stepfather's daughter, her husband and child. His other daughter had the apartment downstairs, along with her family. Our home was across from the roundhouse of the Canadian National Railway. We had to cross many rows of tracks, avoiding the passing trains, to get water and carry it home. I was a frail child and thought my arms would leave their sockets as I carried two buckets of water, especially on washdays when we had to make many trips. We had a little more food than before, as my stepfather was able to find occasional work digging ditches for construction companies. Each day we went along the tracks with buckets to pick up pieces of coal that had fallen from the freight cars. I dreaded this chore, as I would get a sore back from stooping on the tracks, and the coal buckets were very heavy to carry so far back home. I began to experience frequent pains in my right side.

One day at the end of May, I felt a sharp pain in my abdomen, reaching up into my chest. My mother, thinking I had caught cold, gave me two doses of Epsom salts and put a hot mustard plaster on my chest to relieve congestion. I awoke that night in great pain. I called for my mother, but I was so weak she was unable to hear me. I dragged myself to the door of her bedroom and fell on the floor as I knocked. My stepfather grumbled as he set out through the rain to called a doctor at the roundhouse. Mother put me in her bed and applied cold towels to ease the pain. My stepfather came back saying that no doctor was available. At ten the next morning Raymond went for the doctor, who arrived at 5:30 in the afternoon. He found me walking around the house in pain.

When he examined me, he looked very worried; by now my face had turned purple. He ordered an ambulance immediately. I was rushed to the hospital and operated on for a ruptured appendix. The doctor told my mother there was no hope for me. I awoke just long enough to hear her tearful words, "This is my best boy." For five days I hovered between life and death. I suffered much from thirst, for all I was allowed was a wet sponge soaked in ice water, pressed to my lips. I was fed intravenously for many days. Many people, some of whom had never met me, were praying that God would spare my life. I stayed in the hospital 25 days and came to enjoy the good meals and quiet atmosphere as I gradually recovered. I missed Mom and the family, but the love and attention I received from the nurses and the Sisters made me reluctant to go home.

I had good reason not to want to return home. Mr. Melanson began showing an incredible jealousy toward my mother which led to fits of anger. He often beat her, berating the poor woman with harsh words concerning my birth. One of his daughters moved to the city, so we had the flat downstairs to ourselves. The beatings increased with no adults now to intervene. Many times I ran up to him and hit him with my small fists; but a child was no match for his temper and strength. Several times I had to confess that I wished my stepfather were dead so we could live and sleep in peace. The priest could only ask me to pray for him.

In the sixth grade I was taught by a very kindly nun, Sister Eleanor. She soon became for me a guiding hand of God. I tried to hide our family problems from her, but she wasn't easily misled. She often gave me her lunch when I had nothing to eat and arranged to get free milk for all of us at school. She talked with me by the hour, assuring me that someday I would do great things for God and man. She also arranged to get many articles of clothing from a woman whose son was my best pal. With Sister's encouragement, I attended Mass every Sunday and led the younger ones in prayer at home. We said our prayers in secret, because my stepfather now ridiculed us when he found us praying.

During the severe Lenten cold, Syl, Mae and I walked three miles each morning to attend Mass, dressed in summer underwear and flimsy outer clothing. We braved many harsh storms to reach Mass before school began. After Communion we ate cold bean sandwiches in the church basement and then, off to school. At Easter, Sister Eleanor gave me a beautiful basket for my attendance at Mass every day, one of the rare rewards of my childhood.

To keep up with my studies, I had to sacrifice recess time and noon hours to use someone else's books, much to Sister Eleanor's dismay. During my year with her I learned the joys that the practice of the Faith can bring and the strength it gives to help us face the trials of life. She told me one day that in her many years of teaching she had never met anyone as poor as I. But she added, "Roy, someday your ship will come in and we will all be proud of you."

One day, Sister Eleanor urged me to pray that I might know what to do in the future. I made a novena to the Blessed Mother for this intention. On the closing night of the novena, I had a strange dream: the skies opened and at the end of a very bright road I saw the Mother of Jesus walking from heaven toward me. She wore a white dress and veil with a blue sash. In her hand was a glimmering white rosary. As I watched, another road opened, and I saw Saint Bernadette come and kneel before our Lady, holding up her own rosary. I was greatly comforted by this dream, but also bewildered. I related this to Sister Eleanor, who smiled, nodded, and said simply, "They always seem to choose people like you."

4. Be My Son

In the summer of 1937, I visited Mother's sister, Aunt Louise, in a little country village called LeBlanc Office. I stayed there several weeks and during this visit enjoyed good food, country air and lots of peace and quiet. Though not yet robust, I was healthier than I had been for five years. I returned home at the end of August.

I was discouraged at having reached only seventh grade by the age of 15 and fed up with wearing patched "hand-me-downs" that were too big or too small. I decided to leave school and look for work. I was hired as a cobbler's apprentice, working 60 hours a week for five dollars; it was later raised to seven dollars. Victor, the shoemaker I worked for, told me I was lucky to get that! In his native Poland, he had worked just as hard for tobacco money. The shoe-repair shop was in the rear of a clothing store which Victor's wife owned. I was in charge of clerking when we had customers; otherwise, I assisted him in repairing and delivering shoes. To deliver them, I had to buy a bicycle for $29; Victor signed for my payments. We both worked hard and late — I can remember delivering shoes at 1:30 in the morning. I was often stopped by policemen who suspected I was out looking for trouble. I rode through storms, taking many spills on the icy roads to earn my seven dollars.

I enjoyed talking to people in the store and over the phone. Victor seemed to like me, but worked me very hard — much to the dismay and anger of his good wife. She often phoned him at the shop, urging him to let me go home at a decent hour. Once in a while he would soften and pay my way to lunch and a movie. He had a daughter, Mary, about my age, who at times went with me to the show. Her parents confided to my sister Beatrice that they were hoping I would stay on as a cobbler and someday marry their daughter. But my relationship with Mary was one of simple friendship. We both felt we were too young for anything like serious courtship.

Victor's wife had a strong religious influence on me. A member of the Franciscan Third Order, her whole life radiated the humility and charity of Christ, and the spirit of the gentle St. Francis. She called me aside one day and told me that her husband was grossly underpaying me. "He likes you, Roy, in his own way, and you are a comfort to him in his hard work, but he has old-fashioned ideas about teaching trades to young men." She was full owner of their secondhand clothing store,' and she gave me money and clothes occasionally to make up for my low wages. My first Easter with them, she outfitted me with a new blue suit. I felt God had let this happen to me through her so I wouldn't fall into despair after so many years of heartache and insecurity. One day she told me that Christ had done her a remarkable favor; in gratitude, she had promised him to give me a full dinner every day for a month. She often surprised me with new clothes which she bought from the local department stores.

One cold, miserable day, when I was tired and lonely, she gave me my very first wristwatch. It was secondhand to be sure, but it was mine and something I had secretly longed for since I was nine. My mother was also the recipient of many kindnesses from Victor's wife, for I had told her just how much my mother had endured to keep our family together. Burdened with raising our family, Mom had worn herself out seeking help from welfare officials, not only for us but for other poor families. She often gave other starving people half the food she had in the house for us. She told us she couldn't see people go hungry even if our family had to make the little extra sacrifice of sharing with the needy. She was an expert at comforting other mothers and their sick children, and at encouraging wives abused by their husbands. My mother knew what a man's jealousy could do — she had scars to prove it.

One time, I saw my stepfather, in a jealous rage, pick up our little kitten and slam it against the wall of the woodshed. My mother ran after him to save the kitten, but was unable to wrest it from his grasp. Raymond had to end the kitten's pain. My stepfather's cruelty caused me many heartaches. It was terrible to see so much

bitterness and hatred in one man. I prayed every night that peace
would come to our house.

When I poured out my cares to Victor's wife, she smiled encouragement, and in her broken English often prayed with me. I
spent many happy evenings with her family, singing while Mary
played the piano, and dancing to their Polish polka records. On my
16th birthday they showered me with expensive presents; and
when I arrived home, my mother met me with a huge birthday
cake — made with ingredients this kind lady had provided. I
finished the day off by going to a movie featuring Mickey Rooney
and Lewis Stone in the famous "Andy Hardy" series. Andy and his
father talked together as father and son. I watched with avid interest;
the part of the son was symbolic of the life I longed to live with my
unknown father.

For a while I entertained the idea of becoming a lay brother.
I kept this secret to myself until I was 17. When I could no longer
remain passive to the inner conviction that I was meant to work
for Christ, I first told my mother, and then, with Syl, I paid a visit
to my pastor and told him of my desire. He received us warmly and
listened to my dreams. He asked where I wanted to enter and I told
him the Brothers of Mercy, in New York. He asked me many
questions, then told me to come back in a few days. When I returned, he gave me a character reference, with the parish seal on
it, offering the opinion that I would make a good brother. I hadn't
told him that I was illegitimate. I felt that if I did, I would be
committing a sin by talking about my mother and father. There
was a question in the folder from the novitiate asking my father's
name, and I hadn't filled it in for the same reason. I felt that perhaps
when I got to New York I would find some way around my problem.
I was hoping my superiors would like me and give me a chance to
prove myself, and that kindness would somehow conquer the rules
of canon law.

The pastor told me to come back and see him when I was ready
to leave and he would have a check to pay my fare to New York —
and back — if I decided not to stay. When I announced my plans at
the supper table one night, Beatrice started to cry and said I would
cause her a nervous breakdown. She told me I was physically unfit
and that there were other reasons why I should stay at home — chiefly
that Mother needed my help. Many such unhappy scenes followed.
I was surprised to meet such resistance. I wanted to love God so
much, and I felt I could serve him better in a different environment,
apart from persons and places that tended to lead me away from

him. I thought, "Can the desire to become a brother really come from God if it makes people so unhappy and contentious?" Lying in my room, I overheard my mother and sister discussing the matter with visitors. I heard many of them say, "Sylvia, let Roy go. He seems to be meant for something different." My sister remained bitterly opposed.

Mother cried, but she told me they were tears of joy. She said it would break her heart to see me go, but I had her permission. She told me she was pleased that God seemed to want me, considering her past and my status. I loved her more and more as I talked things over with her. She had written to my brother, Fidele, who had moved back to the United States. He had spoken to his pastor, who also advised Mama to let me go.

The whole affair came to a head when I announced that I would be leaving in a couple of weeks. Beatrice began telling me I didn't have the necessary piety — and with this I partly agreed. I had offended God seriously at times, but I wanted to live a better life, placing myself in the hands of those who would lead me to Christ. I didn't really know him, but somehow I felt drawn to love him and I wanted to serve others because of him. In desperation my sister threw a sentence at me that completely broke my spirit and my heart: "When they see your birth certificate, they will send you home!" Together with the memories of my past faults, I took this as a sign from God that he didn't want me in his service.

In a flash, the memory of the day I had found the casket plate came back to torture and humiliate me. My sister was right; I could never be a good lay brother. As my whole life crowded into my memory with all the shame and scorn that had been inflicted on me, I was convinced that no matter how hard I tried, I would end up in hell. The thought, "like father, like son" kept going through my mind; I ran to my room and tore up my application to the novitiate. I never went back to the rectory for the check, nor did I get a chance to thank the pastor. He died shortly after, and I went to church where his body lay in state and asked God to show him mercy and love for his friendship and encouragement.

Months later, I went to the Cathedral one evening for confession. I arrived at midnight — I had just finished work — as the curate was locking the church. I said that I could come back the following week, but he took me by the arm and gently led me to the rectory porch to hear my confession. I went to kneel, but he told me to sit in a rocking chair and relax as I confessed my sins. When I took off my cap, he made me put it back on. He was very good and gentle, and I felt Christ must have been like him. I told him about my frustrated plans to become a brother. He said, "Wait awhile, Roy. Perhaps God has other plans for you." He walked with me to the sidewalk and put his arm around my shoulders, telling me to remain faithful to Christ in spite of the heavy odds against me. I thought perhaps he was just humoring me; I was more and more convinced I was destined to live and die a social outcast. As time went on, I fought less and less as worldly temptations drew me toward a wayward life. I did rouse myself to go to church and pray occasionally, but I didn't put my whole heart into it.

One night, to my discouragement and despair, I had what I thought was my first encounter with the devil. I say "encounter" because until this time he had only indirectly influenced me through other people and events. But this night, as I knelt in the dark church, I had the strongest conviction that the devil was making a personal and direct attack on my spirit. I somehow knew that I was under the influence or persuasion of a spirit that was evil, for there was no one else in the church from whom I could have heard what I heard. I was positive it was not my imagination conceiving the thoughts coming from this evil visitor. What this voice was urging — commanding — me to do was contrary to everything my youthful heart yearned to do and be. I did not hear this voice with my ears, but the flow of words through my "inner ear" was pitiless and unrelenting: "Why don't you face the facts as they are? You are the fruit of sin. God hates kids born like you were. You can never be good. Sin is in your blood. . . ." And he repeated several times, "Like father, like son." The voice continued: "Why don't you enjoy yourself while you have the chance? You are handsome; the girls like you. Give in, live! You know from experience that society hates you and the Church only tolerates you. Think of the pleasures that await you in the world. There is so much to be had. All you have to do is stop hesitating. You have nothing to lose. You have no father; you have nothing; nobody cares for you anyway." This dreadful voice went on and on, overwhelming me with despair. I leaned my head on the pew and wondered what would become of me. I couldn't understand how the devil would be so bold as to harass a soul in the very house of God. I looked toward the Blessed Sacrament and wondered why Jesus wasn't doing something about this unwanted visitor. The crushing weight in my soul brought bitter tears of loneliness and dejection.

Then, in a moment, I was filled with a refreshing peace and joy of heart and mind. I was suddenly aware of Jesus leaning over me. I didn't see him with my eyes, for they were closed and drenched in tears. But in some wonderful way, I saw him standing close to me. I noticed his sandaled feet and the lower part of his robe. For the first time in my life, I experienced Jesus. I knew — *knew* — that he lives and is greatly concerned about people. His presence near me nullified the effect of the earlier visitor and I knew then that these two great spiritual forces were in direct combat over my soul. Jesus told me that his Father loved me. Then I heard him say with very great emphasis (and how pleased I was when he called me by name!), "Roy, you are important to my Father and to me. My Father loves you and I love you, and my Father wants you to be his son." Jesus flooded me with a bright new hope and with deepened insights into the wondrous ways of God. The most exalted words I had ever heard about God were as nothing compared to this experience.

I was now convinced of two things: that there was a God who cared about me, and that the devil is a very active and hateful force in the world. I recognized that the devil is a liar and that man by himself is no match for him. But I was very consoled by the wonderful truth that I learned that night — that the devil is impotent in the presence of the Redeemer. This visit of Christ convinced me that there was something noble and dignified about me as an individual, regardless of my origin and past history. I left the church that night no longer feeling that I was a nobody. I was convinced that Christ saw something good in me, even though I didn't know what it was. Of this I am certain, that after Christ's visitation no one ever again caused me to feel rejected and discouraged by the circumstances of my birth.

I took my time going home, reflecting on what had happened. The words of Christ kept coming back to mind: "Roy, my Father wants you to be his son." "How can this happen?" I asked myself repeatedly. I had always been taught that Christ was *the* Son of God; I had never heard of anyone else being God's son. It was very confusing. When I got home, I went to my room, keeping my thoughts to myself. I was too happy to go to sleep, and I lay there wondering what this could mean. I had the distinct feeling that I had been invited by God to do *something,* but what? If there was anything that matched my moral weakness, it was my ignorance of spiritual things. I simply thanked Jesus for his goodness and told him that I loved him. I had the strongest feeling that my whole being was being drawn by some very powerful and very good force. I knew my life would never be the same again.

5. Pursued and Struck Down

About this time, I made a parish mission given by Passionist priests from the United States. I attended Mass regularly and made an occasional visit to church. However, my brother Raymond and his friends persuaded me to attend parties with them, and I became more and more attracted to the carefree life of the world. I was still haunted by the memory of Jesus' visit; it had placed in my heart a spark of love for a God who cared enough for me to want me for his son. Yet I tried to drown my restlessness in the joys and pleasures of parties and dates, hoping to find the happiness that had eluded me all my life. The time between confessions grew longer, and I drifted from the practice of my Faith. Moral erosion had set in. Easter came and went, and I missed my Easter duty for the first time.

When I turned 18, I joined the local Reserve Army field artillery unit. We had drill sessions twice a week. I made many new friends, most of whom helped to draw me away from my devotional life. I bought an Irish accordion and learned to play jigs and reels. I took it to many parties and dances, and it helped make me popular with other teenagers. This was part of my determination to make people like and accept me. I had several girl friends; but even as I

41

danced in the crowded halls, I was troubled by the desire to enter religion.

At times I was drawn almost irresistibly from places of amusement. I would excuse myself by saying, "I have to be alone," and wander aimlessly along the city streets. I knew something was taking place in my soul. On many of these walks, my memory was filled with the words, "Be my son." But knowing no other life than that of the world, I told myself the idea was crazy. I had never heard of anything like Christ's visit to me, so I tried to put it out of my mind. I tried to satisfy my appetite for happiness; but the more I drank from the barrel of worldly pleasure the more I thirsted for inner contentment. Many times I went to church, intending to confess my sins and direct my life back on straight paths. I would stand in line at the confessional; but, losing my courage, I would find myself back in the street, too ashamed to confess.

I became more and more restless. When Jesus came to me, I knew he was both pursuing me and drawing me toward him like a magnet. Yet I tried to flee from him. I became more deeply involved in "good times." The more I tried to run away from him, the more insistent he became. He pestered me day and night with his hounding presence, constantly calling me to be his Father's son. I remembered the great peace his visit had produced in me, and I knew he wanted me to change my ways — but how? What surprised me was the fact that no matter how much I sinned, Christ continued to pursue me.

One night while listening to the radio at my steady girl friend's house, I felt my mind being drawn by that same compelling spiritual force. I forgot where I was; I could only wonder what God wanted. My girl friend called to me to "come down out of the clouds." She couldn't know that Christ continued to fill me with the peace of his unseen presence. This period of my life was one of bewilderment, astonishment, happiness — and, I must admit — resistance. I wanted to follow Christ in the path he pointed out, but I didn't have the moral strength to turn my back on the pleasures of worldly life. I tried to shake off his advances. I distracted myself, buried myself in artillery studies and tactics. I cooperated with the officers and was made a corporal, a promotion of which I was very proud. I now drilled three nights a week and spent the other nights going to country folk dances, swing-time dances, parties — anything to offset the influence of his presence.

The suggestion, even the conviction, that I was doomed to hell crossed my mind quite often, but it didn't bother me much —

I was having too much fun. But it wasn't enough to satisfy the emptiness in my heart. At night, I still slipped into a church, unnoticed, and knelt in the shadows, crying many tears of shame and sorrow. I was sick of sinning; I longed to return to the days of my innocence. I prayed to God, while at the same time fighting him off. From the tabernacle, he spoke to my disillusioned soul. He told me of his love for me, a love that led him to die on the cross for me. I was comforted by his words and made good resolutions, but still returned to my old ways. I frequently told him he was wasting his time on me, that I was unique as a sinner. He did not give up. Neither did I.

I longed to surrender to him, but what did that mean? My struggle with God went on for three years. I quit my job in the cobbler's shop to work in a grocery store, but my inner conflict remained the same. I began to wonder — since he pursued me day and night — "Why doesn't he make me do whatever he wants?" I was too ignorant of the ways of God to know that he respects the free will of each man and will not force it to act. I told him repeatedly I wanted to be good, without knowing what it meant. I was empty. I knew I was missing something, but I didn't know what. One day I complained to Jesus that I was terribly unhappy, and I begged him to put my soul at peace, no matter what it might cost me. Little did I know that a heavy cross would soon be placed on my shoulders bearing the words: "rheumatic fever" and "inflammatory rheumatism." The old adage was to be proven that "some people never look up until they're flat on their back."

In June, our military unit was ordered to a distant camp for two weeks' training. On the troop train, I was asked to play my accordion. We sang war songs and old-fashioned ballads and had a great time. At camp, army life was a lark. In the evenings when we were given leave, we danced in the streets with the local girls. I was happy and carefree — until one day, while drilling in the fields, I felt weak under the hot sun. An officer told me to sit in the shade. That evening, some of the men urged me to see a camp doctor but I refused, not wanting to be sent home. I felt sore and generally worn out. While riding home at the end of our two weeks, almost everybody was drinking; and I again played the accordion for the men. But this time I felt miserable.

A few days later, at my home, I felt severe pain in my ankles, wrists and knees. My joints swelled, and I had a fever. Along with two of my buddies, I had decided to enlist in the active service; so I went to Dr. James Stewart and asked him to make me well enough to pass my army physical. He took my temperature, examined my limbs, and said, "Roy, your temperature is 103°! For God's sake, go home and go to bed; I think you have rheumatic fever and inflammatory rheumatism."

My condition worsened rapidly. I lost my appetite and became very weak. The swelling in my joints was alarming, and I didn't respond to treatment. The doctor prescribed only aspirin to ease the pain. I heard my mother ask him, "Is it serious?" He told her, "Woman, this kid is going through hell." I suffered greatly from the burning fever, the summer heat and a swarm of flies. I would have felt like a millionaire had someone brought a fan for my room. From my thighs to the end of my feet I was like two big round flaming logs. All my joints seemed pierced with burning spikes. For a long time, I was fed liquids with a teaspoon, because the joints of my jaws were so inflamed I could scarcely open my mouth.

Often, as I lay on my cot, I wondered, "Why did God let me be born?" I looked back on my careless, worldly living and thought, "What a fool I've been! What an empty, wasted life I've had!" I was convinced I would die soon; the grave concern in the doctor's eyes and his hushed conversations with my mother only increased my fears. All the happiness, the bright future I had dreamed of seemed to disappear. Life seemed very short. At first, my friends came to see me, but their visits became less frequent. When they did come, they stood back from my bed, fear written on their faces. I was not a very pleasant sight.

Eventually, I was left alone with my family. They were visibly shaken by what was happening to me. I could see my stepfather's attitude toward all of us mellow. I could tell by his conversations with me that his ideas about God and people were changing for the better. He showed me great kindness as I cried out in pain and despair. He sat by my bed and begged me not to give up. Yet, despite this little thread of human support, my misery so overwhelmed me that I felt God no longer cared. I seemed to be completely abandoned by the Jesus who had for so long pursued me. I was left to myself, very much alone.

One night when the fever was at its worst and I was suffering intensely, someone offered to apply an ointment to alleviate the pain and reduce the swelling in my joints. After it had been rubbed on my legs, my family retired for the night. It took a little while for the ointment to take effect; when it did, it burned severely and raised large blisters all over my legs. I endured the pain in silence as long as I could; finally it became so excruciating that I cried out in agony. With the rheumatism and weakness caused by the fever I was unable to move my body with the exception of my hands, although they, too, were swollen and painful. I tried waving the blankets to cool my legs, but it did no good. I called for help but couldn't make myself heard; my voice was too weak. My brothers' room was too far away, and my mother and stepfather were both partially deaf. Sobbing filled my entire body and tears streamed down my cheeks. Again I felt completely rejected by God and man. I had wandered far from God, and was convinced that this burning torment was a just punishment; God must have grown tired of my ingratitude and insolence. I thought death was near and that this torment was just a prelude to the eternal affliction that awaited me. The prospect of losing my soul filled me with terror. I could not call my family; I could only call upon God.

Years later, I read Psalm 38, which described precisely the misery I had endured and the devouring need I felt at that terrible moment of my illness:

> Yahweh, do not punish me in your rage,
> or reprove me in the heat of anger.
> Your arrows have pierced deep,
> your hand has pressed down on me;
> no soundness in my flesh now you are angry,
> no health in my bones, because of my sin.
>
> My guilt is overwhelming me,
> it is too heavy a burden;
> my wounds stink and are festering,
> the result of my folly;
> bowed down, bent double, overcome,
> I go mourning all the day.
>
> My loins are burnt up with fever,
> there is no soundness in my flesh;
> numbed and crushed and overcome,
> my heart groans, I moan aloud.
>
> Lord, all that I long for is known to you,
> my sighing is no secret from you;
> my heart is throbbing, my strength deserting me,
> the light of my eyes itself has left me.

My friends and my companions shrink from my wounds . . .
And now my fall is upon me,
there is no relief from my pains
yes, I admit my guilt,
I am sorry for having sinned . . .

Yahweh, do not desert me,
do not stand aside, my God!
Come quickly to my help,
Lord, my saviour!

—Jerusalem Bible

The God of mercy heard my feeble plea for help of body and
soul. I suddenly became mindful of the Mother of Christ, recalling
two of the titles given her by the Church: "Comforter of the
Afflicted" and "Refuge of Sinners." I felt my only hope was to turn
to my Mother to plead for me before her Son. Surely she would
be my refuge in this moment of desperation. With all my strength
I cried, "Mary, you know my mother can't hear me, so I burn and
suffer. But you, dear Lady, are my mother, too; you are the mother
of all men. Jesus gave you to us as our very own. I beg you in
your mercy to help me in my sorrow and pain." I asked her over
and over again for help, reminding her that I was alone and completely helpless, physically and spiritually. On the edge of despair,
I began to lose hope even in the Mother of God.

Suddenly, I felt her presence at my side, much as I had become
aware of the presence of Jesus long ago. Our Lady began caressing
my burning forehead with her hand. I felt its imprint; and in that
instant my raging fever cooled, and I was refreshed in body and
soul. I cried out in gratitude and love to her. I told her how sorry
I was for having offended Jesus so many times. I blurted out many
good resolutions and gratefully put my hand over hers. Then I fell
into a deep sleep, murmuring over and over again, "Thank you,
Mother Mary, thank you, thank you."

I learned more about Mary's place in God's plan by this one
experience than any person or book could possibly have taught me.
Before this, Mary had been a remote person to whom I prayed
feebly; now she was real and present, someone whose love I experienced when Jesus sent her to comfort me and rescue my soul.
I now felt this terrible sickness was not unto death but was meant
for my own good and God's glory.

Only one thing troubled me greatly. Why would Mary come to

help someone who was alienated from her divine Son? I began to feel that I might have been deceived by Satan, deluded in my fevered state. Mindful of my great unworthiness, I tried to convince myself that Mary had not come, but I knew I was lying to myself. She had come on an errand of mercy for Jesus; and no matter how I tried to change the truth to satisfy my doubts or my friends' disbelief, the fact of her visit remained.

I concluded that Mary had come not only to relieve my physical pain, but to set the stage for my return to Jesus. But my conversion did not happen overnight. In spite of the fact that Jesus had shown me such love through this visit of his holy Mother, I could not bring myself to amend my life. I knew I needed first of all to talk to a priest and thus place myself before a representative of Christ. But I couldn't overcome the shame and fear that kept me from doing this.

I remained critical for several weeks after Mary's visit. At times I lay very close to death, hearing what was said but unable to open my eyes. In the inner recesses of my soul I was very much aware of my great longing for the forgiving embrace of Jesus. How great this longing was, only God can understand. I begged Mary to obtain for me from her Son the grace of a truly sincere conversion of life.

6. Glimmerings of Light

October 24, 1942, was a wintry day in Moncton. I could feel the wind through the loosely fitted windows of our dilapidated house as I lay in bed. I showed no signs of improvement and was completely discouraged. Around four o'clock I was shaken by the announcement that a priest was making his annual visits on our street and would be at my house soon. I was afraid to face his questions about my spiritual state.

While I wondered what to say, I heard a knock on the door. Knowing who was there, I was filled with deep shame and resigned to a spiritual third degree — I knew how severe some of our priests were. As he entered my room, he smiled warmly and spoke to my mother. Looking over at me, he smiled again. In that instant I became completely unaware of their conversation; my attention was drawn to someone whose voice was very familiar. Surprised and overjoyed, I heard once again the voice of Jesus Christ: "Roy, I am the Good Shepherd; you are my lost sheep. Since you would not come to me, I have come to you. I come to disentangle you from the briars and thornbushes of sin which have trapped you." As he spoke, my soul was freed of the terrible bonds of fear and shame that had kept me from the sacrament of Penance. I'd had no intention of submitting myself to a priest, fearing he would rake me over the coals. But affected by the gently compelling grace extended by Jesus, my eyes filled with tears of repentance.

Once I resolved to bare my soul to this priest, Jesus vanished. The presence of the priest was now a comfort; I knew he had come in Christ's name. Still, I was apprehensive of what he might say when I told him of my waywardness. Jesus understood, but what of the priest who exercised his power? He began, "Well, Roy, what seems to be the trouble?" I braced myself and answered, "Father, God is punishing me for my unfaithfulness," explaining my situation briefly. Fully expecting him to castigate me, I was astonished to hear him say gently, "Roy, God loves you very much!" I remembered the words of Jesus moments before; now his priest was echoing his words. I begged him to hear my confession. I had been drowning in the dark, lonely waters of sin and now the gentle hand of Jesus was lifting me out of those fearful depths. But he said, "Prepare yourself, and I will come tomorrow with Jesus in the Blessed Sacrament. I'll hear your confession and you can receive him." I begged him again to hear my confession, but he smiled and asked me to wait until the next morning.

I felt that Jesus had accepted my sincere sorrow because of the great inner peace that I experienced. I was convinced he had already come into my heart, that he could not wait until the next day. I was, for the first time in three years, a very happy young man. My happiness must have been echoed in heaven — hadn't Jesus said, "What man among you having a hundred sheep and losing one of them does not leave the ninety-nine in the desert and go after that which is lost until he finds it? When he has found it he lays it upon his shoulders, rejoicing; and coming home, he calls his friends and neighbors saying to them, 'Rejoice with me because I have found my sheep that was lost.' Even so, I say to you, there shall be joy among the angels of God over one sinner who repents." I was aware that this peace was of a kind I had not experienced before. Even though I knew my sufferings would continue, I was finding happiness in the idea that I could adore God's justice by accepting pain with patience. I hadn't suspected that one could be so happy amid such physical discomfort. I thanked Jesus for sending me his representative and longed for morning to come, bringing with it the priest and Christ.

The next morning, I asked my mother what feast day it was. She looked it up and said, "It's the feast of Christ the King." As I prepared for Holy Communion, I addressed Jesus as "King of the Universe," thanking him in advance for coming to the slums — the slums of my sinfulness — in search of me. I thanked him for honoring our poor home by his presence and for the graces of this morning.

Mother met the priest at the door and led him to a table arranged
with a crucifix and two candles. I bowed my head as he placed the
Blessed Sacrament on the table, genuflected, and sprinkled us with
holy water. He then asked the others to leave and sat by my bed.
I began, "Bless me, Father, for I have sinned," and opened every
dark corner of my heart to this man who had been given the power
to forgive sins. He raised his hand over me to forgive my sins and
restore the peace of Christ. As he raised the Sacred Host before me
and I looked at Jesus, all the longings of my heart surged to the
fore. The priest fed me with the Body and Blood of Jesus Christ.

He talked with my mother as I made my thanksgiving; then he
came to me and said, "Be at peace, Roy. In all my years as a priest,
I have never heard a more sincere and complete confession." I
smiled, replying that I had been working on that confession for a
long, long time. He asked if there was anything he could do to help
me in any way. I told him how I suffered from cold and lack of
proper diet; many times we didn't have enough money for medicine.
He said he would see if the St. Vincent de Paul Society could make
our lot a little easier. In a few days, he made arrangements to put
both gas and electricity into our house. He brought me candy and
cigarettes and spoke warm words of encouragement. Father sent a
wonderful woman helper who visited me every week to see to it that
I had fresh sheets, pajamas, cigarettes and books. She also arranged
to have some Sisters come to visit me each week. One of them,
Sister Marie Odile, a very friendly nun, really cheered me up as she
spoke of the goodness of God.

As my sufferings continued, my heart weakened under the
strain of the fever and inflammation. Now pardoned for my sins,
I accepted it patiently, for I felt I had it coming to me. Yet being
young and full of dreams, I wanted to be up and around, enjoying
life. Someone suggested that I talk to a priest who was advocating
prayers for the beatification of Brother Andre, who had built a
shrine in Montreal to honor St. Joseph. I asked a friend to send for
him. This priest gave me a small relic of Brother Andre, urging
me to make a novena to him. I began immediately to apply the
relic to my sore body, begging God through the intercession of
Brother Andre to help me regain my health. On Sunday morning,
as my novena came to an end, I heard the church bell announce
the elevation of the Sacred Host at Mass. A voice within me said,
"Roy, look at your knees." I unwrapped the bandages, and to my
amazement the swelling had vanished. I called my mother and
sister. My mother clapped her hands with the simplicity of a child

and wept with joy. She had labored many months, applying hot towels to my knees to reduce the swelling. God had answered the prayers of Brother Andre.

A few days later, Dr. Stewart came to see me. He was surprised at my improvement but would not let me get up as my heart was very weak. He said, "Roy, if you insist on getting up, I will not be responsible for the consequences." I would have to stay in bed until my legs could lie flat on the bed — the tendons had grown taut and I could not straighten them. I began a second novena, then another and another. By the ninth novena, I was discouraged and tearful. Again, I applied the relic of Brother Andre to my heart, knees, and the cords that were tight as steel. Dorothy, my youngest sister (then four years old), asked me one day why I was crying. I told her I had been praying to Brother Andre for weeks, and all in vain. I smiled to see her walk up to his picture and berate him: "You didn't help my brother Roy!" She came to me and rubbed my knees with the relic, assuring me, "Don't cry, he is going to help you."

Apparently, God was moved by this little child's prayer and faith. On Friday night I was saying my night prayers when I heard Dorothy say, "Hello, Brother Andre." Startled for a moment, I continued to pray, thinking it was a childish whim. Then she came to me and declared, "Roy, Brother Andre is here." Her face shone. I sank back on my pillow, weak with fright. I thought he had come to warn me about my death. My mother asked what was wrong; I was so pale, she thought I had taken another weak spell. I told her what Dorothy had said; Mom asked her about it, and she repeated what she had told me. Summoning what little courage I had left, I asked, "Where is he?" "He's standing by the front door," she said. "Tell him to come in," I said. She said in French, "Entrez, Frere Andre." I watched as she seemed to follow him with her eyes to a spot by my bed. I asked again, "Where is he?" She pointed to my bedside: "He's right there." "What does he want?" "He wants to cure you."

For weeks I had prayed to him with these words: "Dear Brother Andre, you know the agony I have endured all these months. You know that along with the pain, I suffer from cold and all other discomforts of poverty. I depend on the St. Vincent de Paul Society for medicine and clothing, but the medicine helps very little. If you were still in Montreal, I couldn't afford to come to you; but now that you have left this world, I believe you are in heaven where nothing is denied you. I know that, if God wills it, you can come to my side to help me. I would like to be healthy and strong again, but I beg most of all, Brother Andre, for the grace to live a good life." Now, indeed, he had come to my side.

Two days later, Dr. Stewart walked in. No one called him; he never came on Sunday. Noticing my surprise, he said, "I just thought I'd drop in and give you a 'look-see.'" He examined my hands, wrists and elbows; pushed my legs down onto the bed; sat me up and listened to my heart; shook his head and listened again. Then he said, "Roy, I can't figure out why, but you are well enough to get up now." I said, "Doctor, God is good. He did this to me." He answered, "Roy, you couldn't find a better doctor than God." I told him how I had prayed for help, and he said, "*Someone* helped; I was sure you would spend the rest of your life in a wheelchair." He shook hands with me and asked me to drop in sometime for a checkup. I told him I didn't know when I could pay him and he replied, "I don't care if you never pay me; I am so happy to see you well! You have been an obedient patient." This good doctor has since died; very often I ask God to bless him for his kindness in those many trying months.

After I had eaten and freshened up, I announced, "The time has come to try my sea legs." When we discovered after several attempts that I couldn't walk a step, the great joy that had prevailed in my home was shattered. My feet seemed to weigh a ton. After sitting in a chair for a while, my family put me back in bed. A few days later, Sister Odile came to see me. She urged me to pray to the Mother of Christ for the grace to walk again and gave me a chair to put in front of me while I practiced standing. At first I was able to drag my feet two or three steps a day, with much pain and more discouragement. For many days we repeated this exercise. It saddened my mother to see me so thin and wasted — I weighed about seventy-five pounds. After each attempt at walking, my mother massaged my legs and thighs until they ached. Soon I could make my way around the house, pushing the chair in front of me, but I couldn't keep my balance without something to hold on to. A neighbor loaned me a pair of crutches.

One day in late winter, the priest who brought me Communion said something very encouraging: "Roy, not only is your body perking up and getting well, but since I have been hearing your confessions and listening to you talk, I can see a new health in your soul." To pass the time, I spent hours reading old Catholic periodicals that Sister Odile had given me. I also read westerns and romance magazines. The latter brought me no peace of soul, and I gave them up at last; but I found myself bored with so many religious magazines. One day Victor's wife came to see me; Sister Odile had told her I was ill. She said that had she known before, she would have been coming to see me all along. She gave me a substantial amount of money, then handed me a little book — another prayer book. I accepted it, not to hurt her feelings. For 10 minutes she urged me to read it, and I nodded. When she left, I put the book aside.

A few weeks later, I was terribly alone with nothing to read but this little prayer book. I picked it up in desperation. It was *The Following of Christ,* patterned after *The Imitation of Christ.* Each chapter ended with a paragraph of prayerful reflections on its contents. I read it for several days, unable to put it down. A sudden change came over me while reading the first few pages. I began to pray in a manner unknown to me before. I felt that a thick wall had crumbled between heaven and me, and I caught a glimpse of the joy of the Christian life. I began to sense my participation in the very life of God living within me, though I couldn't express it, even to myself. I told Sister Odile and she tried to explain it to me. Although I didn't understand it all, I felt drawn more and more to God. One of the chief characteristics of this new awakening was my awareness that the kingdom of God was within me. It was as if I had gone through life as a beggar and suddenly found a fortune in my pocket. I longed to run in the path of God, but I was to learn that I must creep before I could walk and walk before I could run.

During Lent I read *The Better Life,* written by a Franciscan priest. It described how to live the Christian life according to the rule of the Third Order of St. Francis of Assisi, a religious order for laymen who are drawn to Christian perfection while fulfilling their vocation in the world. This was the answer to my prayer. I still longed for religious life, but I felt too much had happened for that to come about. Sister Odile was convinced I had a religious vocation and urged me to look into it. I kiddingly told her, "I would look cute hopping around on crutches seeking the religious garb in a monastery!"

One day the woman whom Father had sent to help me said, "You should come with me someday to the Third Order of St. Francis." Very excited, I told her about the book I had read. She said she could arrange for me to seek admission to the Order. I promised to accept her invitation as soon as I could leave the house. I continued to read *The Following of Christ.* I felt that God was explaining the deep meaning of most of its contents to me. I was sure of this

because I had been very ignorant of spiritual things, and now they
were becoming very real.

One night, during this happy transition in my life, I had a
dream. I was working as a clerk in a grocery store, when two ladies
entered to be waited on. As I turned to greet them, I looked out
the window. To my astonishment, I saw the Mother of Christ
standing on the front steps of L'Hotel Dieu, the Catholic hospital in
Moncton. She held the Christ Child in her left arm. Without a word
being spoken, I was given to know that Mary wanted me to approach
her. I immediately took the apron from around my neck and threw
it on the store counter. The two ladies said, "Aren't you going to
wait on us?" I answered, "I can't. I must go see what Mary
wants." I ran out of the store and raced toward the hospital. I
believe that I would have run through roaring flames to get there, for
I felt myself drawn toward Christ and his Mother by an irresistible
force.

I ran to the step below the one on which Mary was standing
and begged her to let Jesus come down and be near me. He was
wriggling around in her arms as if he wanted to get down on the
ground and walk. I begged her again and again to let me have
him because I loved him. She looked at me and gave me the most
beautiful smile I had ever seen. She relaxed her arm, and as she did,
Jesus slid down the side of her robe, hanging on with both hands
as he did so. He ran to me. My heart was filled with strong sentiments of love and gratitude. He made it clear to me, again without
words, that he enjoyed being near me. He extended his little hands
to me, inviting me to pick him up and hug him. Our Lady looked
at us and seemed very happy.

After a while, I stood up and gazed out toward the horizon into
a vast openness of land. I called out excitedly, "Come, come, Jesus
wants to walk with us!" To my amazement, I saw people coming
toward us from the four corners of the world. My voice seemed to
have reached every country on earth. Streaming toward us were
people of every race and color. There were men and women from
every walk of life, but there was not a clergyman in the crowd.
Among them were the very old, the middle-aged and young children.
Many mothers held children in their arms. Some of those coming
toward us were hobbling on crutches and canes. Then the great
throng began to strike their breasts and cry out for pardon and
mercy. While the crowd moaned, Jesus ran to his Mother. She
stooped down and placed him in her left arm again. When the crowd
saw this, they called to me to beg the Mother of Christ to give him to

them; they wanted to walk with him. They told me they were sorry for having offended God. I said to our Blessed Mother, "Please let him come down and be with these people." She remained silent and clung very tightly to her little Boy.

The idea suddenly came to me to have these people sing Mary's praises, thinking perhaps this would please her and she would listen to our pleas for help. I called out to the crowd, inviting them to sing the "Ave Maris Stella," the traditional hymn of the French Acadians. I had heard it sung in Latin and did not know what the words meant, but I felt that this would please the Mother of Christ. To my surprise, people from every nation and tongue sang this Latin hymn in unison. Here is the English translation of what we sang:

> Hail, thou star of ocean! Portal of the sky!
> Ever Virgin Mother of the Lord Most High!
>
> Oh! by Gabriel's Ave, uttered long ago,
> Eva's name reversing, establish peace below.
>
> Break the captives' fetters; light on blindness pour;
> All our ills expelling, every bliss implore.
>
> Show thyself a Mother, offer Him our sighs,
> Who for us Incarnate did not thee despise.
>
> Virgin of all virgins! To thy shelter take us:
> Gentlest of the gentle! Chaste and gentle make us.
>
> Still, as on we journey, help our weak endeavour,
> Till with thee and Jesus we rejoice for ever.
>
> Through the highest heaven, to the Almighty Three,
> Father, Son, and Spirit, one same glory be. Amen.

As we finished singing this praise of Christ's Mother, she lowered the Christ Child to the ground. He ran to the people and held his arms out to them lovingly. He seemed to take particular pleasure in the little children, who were nearest to him. As he mingled with the people, I turned to see Mary's reaction to the Child's behavior, and only then did I notice that she was dressed as Our Lady of Mount Carmel. She wore a brown robe and a large scapular which hung from her shoulders to within a few inches of the hem of her robe. Her mantle, like the scapular, was ecru in color. Over her head was a loose-fitting white veil, her hair showing beneath it. She wore sandals on her feet.

Without really speaking, Mary gave my mind this message: "The hospital that you see behind me represents the many spiritual ills of my children. The great lamentation from the multitudes shows the intensity of the spiritual diseases that fill the world. I would alleviate the misery of God's family by giving them my Son to be the life and health of their souls. The gift of my Son to you is symbolic of my role in the providential plan of God for the saving of mankind. His walking with you and with these people is an exterior sign of what God would have take place in the souls of men. All mankind must walk before him in spirit and in truth, united to his eternal Son."

I cried out with a loud voice to the people, saying, "Let us sing praise to God for having given us Jesus as our Savior." I invited everyone to sing "Holy God, We Praise Thy Name." The crowds sang with such fervor that the entire world seemed to vibrate from the intensity of the melody. Jesus ran to his Mother and she picked him up. Together they listened to our hymn of praise. Jesus looked serenely upon this great sea of humanity. Mary then turned toward heaven, whence shone a radiance of indescribable splendor. I followed her gaze. The skies parted and a beautiful light emerged. I was given to understand that Mary was contemplating the Most Blessed Trinity, and the happiness on her face told me how pleased she was that mankind was seeking her divine Son. I was also made aware that the greatness of Mary was nothing compared with the greatness of the Triune God whom she was beholding, and that her glory, exalted as it is, is but a reflection of the glory of the Godhead. Mary herself wanted me to know that she is still a creature, that all she has is from God.

Thus ended my dream, and I awakened sitting up in my bed, with the thunderous singing of millions of people still ringing in my ears. Goose pimples covered my flesh, yet I was not frightened. As I sat there in the dead of night, I found myself burning with a desire to do everything possible to bring the whole of mankind to Jesus. Yet, I had no idea of how to go about it. I placed all my trust in the Mother of Jesus, asking her to show me the way I was to walk.

7. My New Life

One day, a Franciscan priest came to visit me. I told this new visitor of my inclination to join the Third Order, and he encouraged me to respond to the promptings of the Holy Spirit. I was fascinated as he told me of the spirit and ideals that filled the heart of Francis Bernadone as he too resolved to tear himself away from the sinful pleasures of the world and the flesh. The priest said that he knew what it was to fight God by living a worldly life. I told him I was disillusioned with my old way of life and regretted my former ill-will toward God.

I was happy to be alive and once more breathe the good fresh air as I hobbled about on my crutches, gazing at familiar scenes. I began most of my days by attending Mass at the Cathedral of the Assumption, well over a mile from my house. I had to stand at the altar rail to receive Communion. Having Christ with me made my long convalescence easier to bear. Each morning after Mass, I made my way to a little shrine of Our Lady of Lourdes in the far corner of a convent garden near the Cathedral. The nuns gave me the freedom of their garden to make a novena to the Blessed Virgin. I returned there to pray long after my novena was completed, hoping that Our Lady would ask Jesus to let me walk without crutches. I braced myself on the kneeler, held up my crutches in front of her statue and with tears running down my cheeks, begged heaven to let me walk and work again.

I should have been grateful even for the ability to walk with crutches; I reflected on this often, remembering that the doctor had thought I would never walk again. One day I told the Mother of Christ that God apparently wanted me to use crutches forever. I resigned myself to his will, trying to be as cheerful as a 21-year-old cripple can be.

On Good Friday afternoon, while I sat on my bed meditating on the death of Christ, I heard my sister call from the front door, "Oh, Roy, look who is coming down the street! Our cousin Evelyn!" I found myself at the front door looking down the street to greet her. I was stunned to hear my mother cry out, "Roy, where are your crutches?" They were still leaning against my bed. Everyone was laughing and crying at once while I walked around the hall showing off my new strength. On a dare from my sister, I stepped down onto the sidewalk to the surprise of my neighbors. I walked up and down the street, then climbed the stairs to a friend's porch and sat down with him, babbling with happy incoherence. My crutches and I were the topic of conversation for many families as they sat around their tables that night. The next morning I walked to church without need of crutches.

On Sunday, June 15, I was invited to be at the Cathedral to enter the Third Order of St. Francis. Still unable to kneel, I stood at the altar rail as the Franciscan who had visited me said to me, "What do you ask?" I answered, "Reverend Father, I humbly ask of you the habit of the Third Order of Penance, that I might more easily obtain eternal salvation." The priest blessed the scapular and cord, then placed the scapular on me saying, "May the Lord clothe you with the new man, who according to God is created in holiness, justice and truth. Amen." Giving me the white cord to be tied around my waist, he said, "May the Lord gird you with the cincture of purity and extinguish in your loins the passion of lust that the virtues of continence and chastity may dwell in you." He then offered me a lighted candle with the words, "Receive, dear brother, the light of Christ as a sign of your immortality. Amen." At the close of the ceremony, he said, "Dear brother, your name in the Third Order will be Brother Anthony." The master of novices approached me and embraced me with the kiss of peace, symbolic of the peace of Christ. Everyone stood to join the priest in singing, "Praise the Lord, all ye nations; praise him, all ye people, for his mercy is confirmed upon us and the truth of the Lord endures forever."

I was escorted back to my seat, where I listened to a sermon on the duties of a tertiary. What a challenge this sermon was! At last

I had found real purpose in existing. I learned from the life of St. Francis and the rule of the Third Order that I could find joy even in the midst of poverty and suffering. After so many years of ignorance about Christian living, God had now given me a simple rule of life that even the lowliest of men could follow in his search for perfection. I left the Cathedral filled with joy and hope, secure in the knowledge that I was now one of thousands resolved to reach out for Christian holiness while remaining in the ordinary walks of life.

I attended classes of instruction in which our novice master taught us how to live the Christian life. We were reminded to wear the brown scapular and white cord, the external marks of our membership in this great Christian army. We were exhorted to recite our little office of prayers in union with the official prayer of the Church and to pray before and after meals as a reminder that all comes from God and as an incentive to live in his presence. The Holy Rule taught us to strive for detachment from any person, place or thing that might be an obstacle in our path toward God.

This rule of life aroused a great desire to know Jesus Christ better. I had plenty of time on my hands during my convalescence, and I spent much of it visiting various churches. I traveled on foot through rain and snow to get to a church, to assist at Mass. Next to my visits to the Blessed Sacrament, the reading of the gospels was the greatest instrument in helping me to find the living Christ. He weaned me away from my former life, drawing me further and further into a spirit of self-denial. I gave up smoking, drinking and attendance at public dances. I was finding happiness elsewhere.

8. Romantic Beginnings

I received word from Fidele and his wife that they were going to send enough money for my mother, Dorothy and me to spend a month of relaxation and rest with them in Thompsonville, Connecticut. I took a walk one afternoon to visit Sister Odile and told her the good news. The nuns made arrangements for me to go to a large department store in Moncton, and the St. Vincent de Paul Society paid the bill which allowed me to get dressed up for our trip. I felt this trip was from the hand of God; even as a little boy in Port Elgin, I had often asked for the grace to go back to the wonderful country that meant so much to me. I'll never forget the joy I felt on the 30th of June as we crossed the border and I saw the first American flag waving briskly in the morning breeze.

Our bus arrived in Springfield, Massachusetts, much earlier than expected. Fidele and Mary had no telephone, so we took another bus to Thompsonville on our own. My mother was amazed as I directed her from the bus station to their home, on the street where we had once lived. She didn't think I would remember after so many years. We settled down for four wonderful weeks of peace.

The next morning, after I had washed, shaved and dressed, I went to the back door and looked out at the familiar neighborhood where I had spent many happy hours. After breakfast, I walked around the neighborhood and renewed old acquaintances. That afternoon Mary took the three of us for a ride around Thompsonville. I pointed out different spots to my mother to show her I still remembered the town. After supper, we sat together talking about old times. Mae and Syl, who lived in a nearby boarding house, arrived to say hello. Syl had a great sense of humor and could always be counted on to liven up a group. It was hot that night, so I took off my shirt. Syl started to laugh, "You have enough scapulars and medals around your neck to choke a horse! What did you do, get religion?" This remark brought a few laughs from the family. I thought this was as good a time as any to explain my conversion to them. I told them most of the story, withholding the strange spiritual experiences that I had received. There were a few embarrassing moments when Syl started to reminisce about some of the wild times we'd had back home in Moncton. I found it very unpleasant to recall these scenes, but I offered my embarrassment as a sort of penance for my past. Syl asked, "Didn't you get enough religion in the orphanage? I got enough in those three months to last me a lifetime!"

Syl went across the backyard and borrowed an accordion, and I played for the family. We sang old songs until midnight. After Syl and Mae had left, Mary, Fidele, my mother and I sat around the kitchen table. Mary asked my mother point-blank, "Whatever made you adopt Dorothy when you were 50?" My mother explained that a priest from the Cathedral parish had brought her to us when she was three months old, asking us to keep her until the parish found a home for her. She had been put into a Protestant orphanage as an infant, and a couple had taken her to live with them but, because of their drinking and disorderly life, they were not good foster parents. Around midnight one night, someone heard a baby crying in a downstairs tenement, looked in, and found a child lying on a mattress on the floor. This person called the police, who found the tentative parents were out on the town, drinking. The child was taken from them. The orphanage officials, knowing she was of a Catholic family, notified the pastor of the Cathedral parish, who had made the arrangements with my mother to place her with us temporarily. Three weeks later, unable to find anyone who would take her, he asked my mother to consider keeping her. He assured her that the parish would see to it that the child never wanted for food or clothing. My mother asked us all what we thought. "Something keeps telling me to keep this little girl," she said. We all loved her very much by this time and promised to see to it that "little Dot" would never be without a family again.

When Mary heard all this, she said, "Well, there's a lot of talk going around Moncton, from what I hear through letters, that Dorothy belongs either to Beatrice, Mae or one of the boys." My mother got angry at this remark. I tried to calm her, telling her that I, too, had heard such rumors but had decided not to speak to her about them. She started to cry, saying, "How can people be so mean when other people try to do good for others?" I told her, "Mom, you and I and all of us know why we gave Dorothy a home, love and affection. All you have to do is tell yourself that you took her in the name of Christ, who said, 'Anyone who receives a little child in my name, receives me.' " Mary obviously regretted bringing up the subject. I wasn't too surprised by her impetuosity; at different times she had taken me aside to discuss the circumstances of my birth. She was very good-hearted but stepped on the sensitivities of others. After that conversation, Mary couldn't do enough for little Dot. The next morning, Mary asked if I would like to go to Springfield to meet her cousin who was coming to visit her. She laughed and said, "This could mean some dates for you while you're down here, you know." I replied, "I'm not about to go out with an old maid." She asked, "What makes you think she's an old maid?" I said, "Well, if she is your cousin — you're 38 — she can't be too young!"

At the bus depot, we met her cousin Irma — one of the most attractive girls I had ever seen. She wore a while pillbox feather hat, and I remember that she carried a plastic pocketbook made up of black and white squares. Irma had a very sophisticated air about her, and, not being familiar with this type of girl, I said to myself, "She's probably very stuck-up. If she finds out where I come from and where I live, she won't consider going out with me." That evening, as we sat together over a cup of coffee, I learned that you can never judge a book by its cover. Irma was warm and friendly and a very understanding person. I found her easy to talk with, and I didn't wait long to ask her for a date.

On our first date, we joined our hosts and several friends in visiting various night spots in the area. It was good to be out where there was excitement and activity. The next morning, Irma and I attended Mass together for the first time. After dinner, we took a long walk by ourselves and did some serious talking. I told her about the Third Order of St. Francis and how I hoped to follow its rule for the rest of my life. She listened very intently; she had never heard of the Third Order. This was our first opportunity to be completely alone and it gave us a chance to find out about each other. I learned that she was 22, had a good-paying job in the Waltham Watch Factory and no steady boyfriend. I told her I had given up my girlfriend a month before.

Irma was the first girl to whom I could talk about some of my inner hurts and yearnings. We enjoyed being together and took care not to be surrounded by the rest of the people at our house. We went to the movies a few times, then we walked around town while I pointed out many boyhood scenes, including the two schools I had attended. When her week's vacation was over, she surprised me by saying that she was going to telephone her mother to say that she was staying another week. While she was calling, I asked Mary why she had changed her plans. She looked at me and grinned, "What do you think?" I didn't know what to think. I wasn't about to let myself get emotionally involved with any girl at this time, because my future was uncertain and I was out of work. In the week that followed, while Irma and I never openly admitted how we felt about each other, I at least felt that our interest in each other was something more than friendship. But I was determined not to let it be any more than a summer romance.

One day Syl said to me, "You had better watch out; that matchmaker Mary will railroad you into marrying her cousin." I laughed, because I had been watching Mary maneuver us together. One night, after the family had gone to bed, I was sitting at the kitchen table, watching Irma put up her hair. Before either of us knew what was happening, I held her in my arms, kissed her, and told her I loved her. In that kiss I found out that she loved me. Our blissful silence was soon broken by voices in the bedroom off the kitchen. I heard Mary telling my brother in French, "He kissed her, he kissed her!" Fidele laughed and said, "Lie down, you nut, and go to sleep." Irma and I joined in the laughter. I walked into their room and said, "Why, you son of a gun, you've been spying on me!"

When Syl heard the news, he roared in laughter and shook his finger at me saying, "I told you so! I told you!" Mary, more practically, suggested that after I got back to Moncton, I should apply for a visa and return to live with her and Fidele. This seemed to please Irma. I said only, "We'll see. Maybe." When her visit was ended, we were driving her to the bus station when Irma made me promise that we would all come to Waltham for a weekend at her mother's house. We — I — happily agreed to do so.

A week later, Irma's mother welcomed us warmly and introduced us to Irma's family: her sisters, Dora and Edith, and two brothers, Leo and Blair. Our mothers had wonderful talks about Canada, for they had both spent their childhood near Cape Bald, New Brunswick. When we parted Sunday night, Irma and I promised to write each other, and she told me she would welcome another visit from me.

My mother and I spent the next few days packing and organizing our papers for the trip back home. Beatrice had written that she and Pop were doing fine, and that they missed us. Mary tried to persuade me to have my visiting permit extended, but my mother didn't seem too pleased with the idea. She told me she didn't feel like traveling all the way back to Canada with little Dot all by herself. Anyway, I was anxious to get back to a slower pace of living, for I was feeling very tired. When we were about to leave for the terminal, Mary said to me, "Don't forget this," and handed me a picture of Irma. As I boarded the bus, I thanked Mary and Fidele for everything they had done for the three of us. Riding along in the night I thought to myself, "I wonder where I go from here?"

9. Something for Others

We arrived home on July 30. For several days I suffered severe physical exhaustion which seemed to grow worse no matter how much I rested. My stepfather sent me to a doctor, and I gave him the history of my illness. He gave me a complete physical then startled me by saying, "Young man, if you don't get out into the country air and get lots of food and rest, I'm afraid you won't be around to celebrate Christmas." I told him I had hoped to go to work and he said, "Even with the rest I'm recommending, I doubt very much that you could work for a year." He gave me several prescriptions and enough vitamins to last me a couple of months and ordered me to find a place to go as soon as possible. My mother's sister, Louise Richard, urged me to come to her farm where I would be welcome to stay as long as I wished.

The day before I was to leave, I had a new visitor who temporarily altered my plans. For years he had not been a practicing Catholic, and he was only recently discharged from the city hospital. After having some teeth extracted, he drank an alcoholic mixture which proved to be poisonous, infecting his mouth and his entire circulatory system. He lay near death for weeks and had received the last rites. His neighbors offered many prayers that he might be spared to raise his nine children. The doctors said that his jaw wouldn't heal until certain portions of infected bone fell out. He had a large incision on the outside of his jaw. After hearing his story, I asked what I could do for him. He said, "Roy, I heard that the Virgin Mary helped you when you were sick. Would you go to church with me and make a novena to her, to help me become a better man?" I was very surprised at his confidence in me. I told him I was ready to leave on a vacation that was absolutely necessary. He begged me to wait for just nine days. He said, "I don't have the courage to face people looking at me; I haven't been to church in years." I thought for several minutes then told him I would stay home, and take him to Mass and Communion the next morning. We would ask our Lady to intercede with God that he would soon be in good health and able to work and lead a good life. Each morning as we walked to and from Mass, I encouraged and counseled him in the way of the commandments and told him of the joy I had found in serving God. He seemed very eager to follow this advice. He was in his early 50's; I found it strange that I, at 22, was counseling someone more than twice my age. He took a lot of kidding; his friends accused him of being religious only to "get something" out of God. His morale often needed bolstering.

On the last day of the novena, he pounded wildly on our front door, waking everybody up. As I let him in, he opened a piece of gauze and showed me the pieces of bone the doctor had been waiting to see. He was very excited, and so was I. He had nothing but words of praise and thanks for God and the Blessed Virgin as we closed our novena with Mass and Communion. His surgeon told him that now the incision would heal and he could go back to work. This happened over 20 years ago. He has remained faithful to God, and over the years has often repeated this story of God's goodness.

On August 16, I sat in the small bus headed for the country, very grateful for the much-needed rest and relaxation ahead of me and the chance to be alone, for I had a lot of thinking to do. I had been writing to Irma and in our letters we seemed to be drawing ever closer to each other.

Few places on earth mean as much to me as the tiny village of LeBlanc Office, in a secluded, rural part of Canada. There I received some of my most tender consolations from almighty God. It was 42 miles from Moncton, and even before I arrived, I began to experience a wonderful change in the air. The bus stopped at the foot of a hill. At the top of this beautiful green prominence stood a tiny white country house. Aunt Louise came to the gate to meet me, receiving me very warmly and promising to do everything in her power to make me strong and well. Her husband, Uncle Paul, was a semi-invalid, crippled for years with rheumatoid arthritis, who spent most of his time in a rocking chair. When he did walk, he had to lean on two canes. He told me, "We'll fatten you up, boy, we'll fatten you up!" They gave me a tiny garret room facing east; from it I could see the entire village of farmlands — there were only about 20 families. The village had received its name from my grandfather and his brother, who had built most of the houses. My room had a refreshing fragrance; I found this came from the mattress, a tick filled with fresh straw. I had brought my accordion, and that first evening I played for my hosts while they sang some French-Canadian songs dear to the Acadians.

I woke the next morning to the warm, bright rays of the sun. I stood at the window and inhaled the wonderful air. After breakfast, I was out weeding the strawberry patches with Aunt Louise, who was very happy to have an extra hand with the farm chores. I scrubbed floors, painted and helped with the dishes. She told me about her own hardships as a child and how my mother had left home at age 11 because of difficulties with her stepmother. By the age of 12, she was working for a living in St. John. She told me that she and my mother's father were very sorry they hadn't shown my mother more kindness at the time of my birth. Uncle Paul, a proud and righteous man, said he had no use for people who had lost their honor. Aunt Louise shook her fist at him saying, "Old man, you have a lot to learn."

She insisted that I drink at least a pint of warm milk fresh from the barn every day. She said after a few days, "Already you have a nice healthy color to your cheeks, Roy." Within two weeks I began to feel stronger. My aunt and uncle retired at eight-thirty every night and were up at five in the morning. Alone in the evening, I had a chance to think and relax while I played the Victrola. I spent these leisure moments reading the gospels, a book I had received from a priest friend with whom I had discussed my vocation. He asked me to read the scriptures every day and also gave me a commentary on the gospels put out by the Young Christian Workers Movement. By reading Christ's life, I soon began to see him, as it were, walking across the pages of scripture. Not knowing what meditation was, I nevertheless formed the daily practice of thinking about Christ and trying to act like him. I soon found myself becoming a new person. I began to feel I had been born again and was now living a completely new life based on the person and actions of Jesus Christ.

With each passing day, my love for him grew stronger, springing from the wonderful realization of his tremendous love for me. The house had a sort of monastic atmosphere, and in this quiet, so close to nature and its Creator, I derived a benefit far superior to my pleasant activity in the noisy city, surrounded by my boisterous friends.

I missed going to Mass and Communion each morning; the church was several miles away. On Sundays we had a ride from a neighbor who drove to church with a lumber truck full of townsfolk. When we arrived at church, our clothes were completely covered with dust from the roads. The white parish church was typical of the beautiful churches in the New Brunswick countryside. It was a pleasure to assist at Solemn High Mass and hear the wonderful choir of men and women from the farms singing hymns in our native tongue, hymns I had often heard my mother sing. I made many friends, some of whom invited me to their homes for dinner or supper.

I was walking home one bright, sunny day along a dusty road, holding my rosary in my hand as I recited the prescribed prayers for the Third Order of St. Francis. I was stopped dead in my tracks by a wonderful spiritual experience. It was a moment of great awe; the veils of nature were pulled aside and I was made aware of the magnificent power of God underlying all things — indeed, the secret of life itself. Never before did nature have this impact on me. I was filled with great peace and joy, for I sensed the presence of God in everything. This moment gave me a new strength of heart, mind and spirit. It was wonderful to be alive in this world. Life took on a larger and deeper meaning, and I thanked God for having placed me on this earth. For the first time in my life I was grateful for the sunshine, the grass, the flowers, the animals — for everything my eyes beheld and my human nature enjoyed. They meant all the more to me as I was shown in a mysterious manner how God sustains and conserves these things by his presence. I don't know how long I stood there, but I do remember that this experience took my breath away momentarily, and it was several minutes before I was able to breathe regularly again. From this experience I learned also the sacredness of work, rest, recreation, yes, and even storms, for they no longer depressed me as they used to. This was the first time that I ever really adored God in nature. I felt very close to the Creator whose hand had fashioned these gifts and whose love had poured into them so much beauty and goodness. I told my aunt and uncle about my experience and was told, "Roy, you should be a priest." It was strange that they mentioned this; I had begun to feel the old desire to consecrate myself to God in his service. Several nights later, I talked to my aunt about becoming a brother. She said, "Roy, don't go lock yourself up in a monastery; it's too hard a life."

One Sunday morning, while kneeling in the front seat of the church, I noticed a man in the sanctuary whom I took to be a priest. I didn't pay much attention to him, but later in the week, while visiting my Uncle Adolph in another part of town, I saw this same man coming toward the house. I retired to the bedroom; I didn't feel like talking "high-class French" to anyone that day. I heard him ask, "Who is that fellow that ran away?" My uncle called me out to introduce us. He was not a priest but a seminarian. When I told him why I had gone to the bedroom, he assured me that he spoke English, and we chatted for a while. Soon after he left, I began to walk back to Uncle Paul's and was surprised to see this young man waiting for me. I asked why he was waiting, and he said, "I was hoping you would be coming out." "Why?" I asked. "I've been wanting to talk to you about spiritual things. There was something in your manner of praying that attracted me." He asked if I would spend a few days with him at his parents' home in the next village. I agreed.

The next Sunday, he introduced me to his parents and his family. He led them in the rosary; then the two of us went upstairs to his bedroom. He closed the door and said, "Roy, I want you to try on my cassock and Roman collar. Somehow I think you were made for one of these." I was surprised, for I hadn't told him about my longing for the religious life. I was happy to try them on. When I saw myself in the mirror, a lump came into my throat. He urged me to talk about Christ, the world, people; we talked until five in the morning. He seemed to want to know what made me tick. I told him the things I would do if I were a priest: how I would try to be like the Christ who had come to me and showed me his wonderful characteristics and the power that radiated from him as our Savior. I told him I loved people because Jesus loved them.

During our two days together, we drove around the village in his father's horse and buggy, talking about God. The morning I was to leave, he called me to one side and said, "I'm going back to the seminary; but I want you to know that I am going back to be ordained a priest of God next year in great part because of you. I was determined before I saw you in church not to finish my studies for the priesthood." I felt very humble before the Christ who I knew was entirely responsible for the help he had received. He said, "Whenever you bless yourself, remember that it was the reverence and love you showed for the Blessed Trinity that attracted my attention and made me want to see you, and that our visit together saved my vocation." I laughingly told him, "Well, from now on you will be my personal priest." He encouraged me again to give serious thought to the priesthood as there was a great need for priests. I just told him that I didn't think I would ever become a priest. I thanked him for the wonderful visit, and he promised to write.

A few nights later, a friend of my aunt came to visit, leading her elderly blind husband. I was sad to see a man unable to enjoy the things my eyes could contemplate. When he spoke mournfully of his blindness, I suggested that while God may allow a man to lose his eyesight, even the blind have the wonderful opportunity to see God with the eyes of faith. He told my aunt that I had lifted his heart more than I could realize. He made me feel I had done something for another man. He and his wife stayed the night, and my aunt told me later that her blind friend had heard me saying the rosary in my room and knelt to say it with me.

As I worked in the fields and around the barn, I grew conscious of an interior conversation between Christ and myself. He unfolded to me the beauties of the interior life of man with God. I felt the desire for a closer imitation of Jesus. I wanted to keep chaste and develop strong moral habits, not because I feared hell, but because I loved God. Jesus taught me that in Baptism I had become a God-bearer, and I began to notice the influence that the presence of Jesus in me was having on others with whom I worked and spoke. I felt more and more that I should become a lay brother to win souls for Christ and for his Father, so I stopped writing to Irma. I still loved her, but I was also attracted to the religious state. Even if ours was more than a summer romance, I didn't think she would consent to share my life of poverty. So I didn't feel guilty about not writing.

For several weeks I was unable to go to Sunday Mass for lack of a ride. My longing for the Eucharist was so acute that I couldn't look towards the church steeple without suffering from the deprivation of God in my heart. I made spiritual communions throughout the day, begging Christ to fill me with his presence and to let me continue to change my way of life. After several weeks of this privation, Jesus took pity on me. As I lay on my bed, I had another mysterious dream. I saw the Blessed Sacrament in a monstrance placed in Aunt Louise's sink, surrounded by stacks of dirty dishes. I was appalled to see this great memorial of Christ's love so neglected and ignored. I set about making an altar on the sink board with linens, flowers and candles. I went to Aunt Louise's door and called out toward the road, and many young men came into her kitchen to kneel in adoration with me before Jesus Christ.

In this dream, I saw myself directing many young men to the sacrament of Penance; they later returned and knelt with me in adoration. While kneeling before the Good Shepherd, concealed under the appearance of bread, I saw the Blessed Sacrament enlarge and begin to shine with a radiance I had never seen before. Suddenly the species of the Blessed Sacrament dissolved and I saw the person of Jesus Christ — the Word of God made man. This startled me so much that I awoke and sat up in bed; and before me stood the same Jesus Christ. I held out my arms to him, and he gave himself in Holy Communion. He entered my flesh in the same mysterious manner in which he had passed through the door of the upper room where his apostles were in hiding after his death. Then he made me aware that he had come to me in answer to my sincere hunger for him, the food of my soul. By this wonderful favor, he opened my mind to many truths concerning his presence among men in the sacrament of his love. I received this Holy Communion with great fervor, humility and gratitude. I knelt on the floor, and for two hours expressed my love for God who was so mindful of my needs and longings. For his part, Jesus impressed upon my mind that I was to bring many men to him through the sacrament of his love, but he didn't say how or where this would come about.

While this wonderful grace strengthened my soul, I also noticed great improvement in my physical well-being, which caused Uncle Paul to say, "We have fattened up our young steer." Early in October, I decided to return home. Uncle Paul and Aunt Louise begged me to stay through the winter, but I thought it wiser to go back home and be near a doctor, should the need arise. As I left this wonderful couple, they cried like children. On my way back to Moncton, I thought of the good God who had planned such a fine country retreat for me and who was sending me back stronger not only in body, but in spirit. After I arrived home, I visited the doctor. He examined me completely and shook his head as he said, "I don't know what happened to you out there, but if you want to, you can go to work tomorrow; I think you are going to be all right."

10. Uncertain Steps

While waiting for a job opening, I received another letter from Irma, asking why I hadn't written for so long. I didn't know what to say, so I didn't answer. I was doubtful about religious life, yet I couldn't ask Irma to marry me no matter how much I loved her, because I was unable, so I thought, to offer her a legal name. I knew from stories I had read that many girls would not marry a man who was illegitimate. I made up my mind to lead a single life in the world as a Franciscan tertiary.

I found work in the shipping department of the Royal Canadian Air Force Equipment Depot in Moncton. The job paid well, but it was heavy work. I attended daily Mass and received Holy Communion. From the Eucharist I was certain I received new strength to rise above my old ways. Some friends who had known me well in my reckless and carefree days didn't for an instant believe I would persevere in my new way of life. In my scrupulosity, I believed what I heard, that I would soon go back to my old ways. The thought of doing so made me afraid and I increased my visits to Christ in the Blessed Sacrament. I would kneel in tears begging him for the strength to keep the commandments and remain loyal to him.

I found much strength and hope in making the Way of the Cross every day. At times, while meditating at the stations which show Jesus fallen under the crushing weight of our sins, I heard him speak to me inwardly, "Learn from this event in my Passion that as I rose again after each fall, you, too, must take courage and rise from your spiritual weakness and follow me to the hill of Calvary where I was crucified for you. I want you to learn perfect self-denial in which you will crucify your self-will and your natural tendencies. By doing this you will glorify me and someday you will join me in the glory of my resurrection."

Some friends and neighbors, seeing my visits to church, smiled complacently as if to say, "Wait and see — he'll soon give up." I was called a hypocrite and other unkind names to discourage me from following Christ. It seemed that nearly everyone I spoke with, even members of my family, doubted the sincerity, or at least the finality, of my conversion.

One afternoon after visiting the Blessed Sacrament, I went down to the crypt where the first Archbishop of Moncton is buried and prayed to him, asking him to pray for me. I knelt on the concrete floor beneath a large crucifix, in spite of the discomfort to my still sensitive knees. I reminded Christ of what people were saying, of their suspicions about my perseverance and my fear their predictions might come true. I fully realized how easily I could leave him. I raised my head to look at him, telling him he was the only one who seemed to believe me, asking him to trust my sincerity. As I begged for courage, to my wonderment and joy, the head of Christ shone with a glorious brightness that lit up the corner of the crypt; his head bent forward and his arms left the cross to reach out and embrace me. Jesus made me realize that he suffered and died so sinners would find new life, hope, strength and courage.

I no longer cared what people thought of me, good or bad. There was an understanding between my Savior and me; that was all that mattered. As time went on, Jesus helped me to understand the full meaning of the ten commandments. I came to realize how terrible sin is and made fresh attempts to live according to the will of God, expressed in these commandments and in the precepts of his Church. Every evening I examined my conscience in the new light Jesus had revealed to me, to see how I had lived that day. He taught me to turn my eyes from anything that might lead me to sin. I learned to measure my words; and whenever I heard anything that might turn me from Christ, I made acts of love for him. He told me that whenever I was tempted by impurity, I must look for him in the souls of others. I soon found myself adoring Christ in everyone and revering the human body as I had not done before.

Though I attended movies, went bowling and visited friends, I found myself thinking more and more about Irma. I hadn't written her for some time, yet I found myself loving her more and more. I could scarcely look at her picture without longing to have her as my wife. Unknown to me, Irma's mother had discovered the circumstances of my birth and told Irma, "Perhaps that is why Roy hasn't written." She urged Irma to burn some candles before the statue of Our Lady and pray that she would bless our romance. I wrote after several weeks, telling Irma as tactfully as I could why I had not written. She and her mother discussed my letter, and Irma wrote me that they would be in Moncton for a month's visit in January. I asked God to help us find a way around what was to me a very big problem.

11. Strength from Above

After my enthusiastic beginnings in the spiritual life, I learned that the struggle to imitate Christ and remain united to him is something that goes on every hour, every day. Often, after Communion, Christ filled me with joy and peace. Yet I had to be on my guard to keep up my inner struggle while living and working with people who were content to have a good time. I soon found that I had to rein myself in to remain loyal to God. There were times when my hunger for self-gratification was so powerful that, to overcome it, I had to kneel for hours with my arms extended, begging Christ to help me crucify my self-will and my wayward faculties. Though the fight was long and painful, the peace I felt after each victory made it well worthwhile. God opened new horizons of the spirit for me, but he did not stifle the cries of my lower nature.

The devil was not idle during those early months of my conversion, as I fought with enthusiasm against my past bad habits. I feared nothing more than rebellion against God, knowing it would rob me of all the riches I had gained. Sometimes the only thing that kept me from giving in to temptation was fear of God's anger. Little did I know then that "the fear of the Lord is the beginning of wisdom." At times I took pride in my new spiritual strength; pride led to carelessness; and carelessness, on a few occasions, to a fall. I knew enough to tell Christ I was sorry, but I was not yet used to his instantaneous mercy.

The devil often taunted me about free will, which separates men from the rest of earth's creatures. He said to me: "I know your tendencies; I can afford to wait for the right moment. . . . Go ahead, enjoy this Christ of yours — I'll have your soul yet, wait and see. . . . You will follow your own will someday. . . . This way of life is for the strong, not for you." His words filled me with confusion and fear.

One day a friend repeated a remark made by our pastor, "It's too bad that Roy lives down on the Bowery." He feared I would never be able to rise above these circumstances. So did I. I told Christ that I felt he was wasting his time on me — even his priest doubted that I would ever amount to anything. The meetings of the Third Order sometimes depressed me because all the other tertiaries seemed to me to be so close to God. I felt they had made a mistake in letting me enter their fraternity. Yet I kept hoping in the strength of Christ who alone can read the hearts of men. I begged him to let me die rather than offend him seriously. I was so ignorant of God; had I known scripture, I would have known that when God begins a work, he will also bring it to perfection.

One night he came to my assistance in a very striking manner. Just before leaving the house for the movies, I knelt on one knee and said, "Holy Spirit of God, enlighten and help me." I meant this to be only a quick prayer, but God had other ideas. Suddenly I felt that a powerful, living force was hovering over my head. I knew beyond any doubt that I was under the influence of the Spirit of God, making his presence as a Divine Person known to me. I cannot adequately describe how I knew it was he; I only know that in some mysterious manner my mind had recognized him. He was invisible, yet he filled me with a strong, person-to-person love. And I saw — again, without seeing — the awesome chasm between the fire of God's love and my puny capacity to receive it. When the first waves of God's love enveloped me, I thought I had received all that God had to give; but this all-powerful Spirit moved with even greater loving force until I feared that I would die of joy. I raised my hands over my head and, completely oblivious to my surroundings, cried out, "O Lord, enough! I cannot stand any more! O my God, I love you!" I rose from my knees, intoxicated with the wine of the Spirit.

On my way downtown, I stopped at a church to thank Jesus for this wonderful grace. Expecting to find the church in darkness, I was surprised to see a large crowd gathered for a novena service. I was more surprised to hear the preacher's words: "Friends, I want to talk to you about the Holy Spirit of God. If you but knew the love that this Holy Spirit has for each of you! The strength of his love for you is so great that if he ever let it flow on you with all of its eternal power and depth, you would die from joy." My heart burst with gratitude to God and tears flowed. I was convinced that Jesus had sent the Holy Spirit, the Third Person of the Blessed Trinity, to guide me on the path toward God. I was so filled with joy that I no longer wanted to attend the movie; I returned home and spent the whole evening in prayer and solitude.

From that day on, I was acutely aware of the Holy Spirit living in me. I had been largely ignorant of the Church's teaching about this Person of the Blessed Trinity. I had thought about him in preparation for Confirmation when I was nine, but had not grasped the full meaning of the Holy Spirit's role in my life. Now, however, my relationship with God was transformed. I often knelt to adore God living within me, or entered into a silence in which God and I loved each other without words. He opened up new horizons of the spiritual life undreamed of by my untrained mind; his outpouring of grace made me soft and pliable in his hands, and in time I came to obey his promptings easily and without hesitation. I felt a new security in my attempt to live a good life. He gradually filled my mind with the wonderful treasures hidden in the teachings of Jesus Christ.

As time passed, I became conscious of saying extraordinary things about God when I attempted to lead others to him, things that I knew did not come from the limited knowledge I had acquired. I was surprised when priests and well-trained religious told me that my thoughts about God were confirmed by the teachings of Sacred Scripture and of Tradition. Often the Spirit would say to me, "I have loved you with an everlasting love"; I was much consoled, later on, to find these words in scripture. This Holy Spirit aroused in me a burning desire to draw other souls to almighty God. In my first attempts to do so, I invited people from my street to recite the rosary with me every evening before the statue of the Sacred Heart of Jesus. I had to exercise the greatest restraint not to stand on street corners and sing out the praises of God to all who passed by.

In the confessional one night, I mentioned my ambitions to a priest. "I feel as though God wants me to work for him and to win souls, but I don't know what to do." He said, "Remain loyal to God, continue as before. When God wants something done by you, he will make it known in unmistakable terms." I left the church that night fully determined to place all my trust in the Divine Comforter and Counselor. I would rely totally on the power, love, wisdom and strength of this Guest of my soul. My reliance on him for everything soon became as natural to me as breathing. I found that he was establishing a wonderful harmony in all my attempts to honor God in thought, word and deed. I could not adequately thank him for living within me, acting within me, showing me the way to lead others to him.

I was also grateful to this Spirit for teaching me how to love and cherish the splendid grace of solitude, wherein God and the soul can converse alone. I told my friends that I carried heaven within me. The Holy Spirit showed me an indescribably comforting spiritual life going on within me. Many commented on my attitude when speaking of God, praying, and assisting at the Church's public worship of God. This I attributed to the Holy Spirit who personally taught me reverence toward himself.

He taught me also the inner meaning of the greatest commandment of all — that I should love God with my whole heart, mind, strength and soul, and my neighbor as myself for the love of God. This wonderful commandment became a shortcut to keeping all of God's commandments. I found as I strove to keep it that obedience to the other commandments followed almost as a matter of course. I was so aware of his presence in me that everything I did took on a new meaning, as I began to look at things from God's point of view. Many things that I had thought were so wise and prudent from a human standpoint, I now knew to be foolish in the eyes of God.

This Spirit made me fully aware that I as a person — body and soul — was regarded by God as someone sacred. Not only did the Holy Spirit open my mind to the meaning of man's love for God, but he also made me appreciate the mutual love of a man and a woman which ideally flows from their love of God. As I read the teachings of the Church on the holiness of the married state, my heavenly Counselor filled my mind with the sacredness of sex. I no longer regarded sex as something "dirty," but as a wonderful gift from God to be used according to his plan for mankind. He took away all desire to enter the religious state, and I found myself yearning to have Irma as my wife so that our human love could find fulfillment in each other and in Christ. I could hardly wait for the day when we might see our love bear fruit in children; our children, God's children. In my letters to Irma, I wrote of many of these thoughts and hopes. Much to my surprise and joy, her thoughts were like mine. I prayed for the grace to live this wonderful sacrament and to love and respect this holy state as Christ does.

The divine Spirit also erased from my mind the fear of death; he made me know that he was with me in all my activities, that he was the support on which my very life rested. I felt that when the time came to give an account of my life, this wonderful Friend would accompany me to the throne of the Father. He had a calming, stabilizing effect on my emotions and helped remove all inclinations to resentment, bitterness and anger toward those who had contributed to my unhappiness in the earlier part of my life.

What I especially liked about my association with the Spirit of God was that it was hidden from the eyes of everyone else. Every man, after all, is an island — and on this island lives the Holy Spirit. Knowing that this powerful, wise, loving and understanding Spirit lived in me had another wonderful effect upon me. It freed me from all the fears that had resulted from the many unhappy experiences in my boyhood. The only fear he left me was the fear of offending so good a God. But it wasn't a cramping fear; it was a spur to love.

He commanded me to search the scriptures that I might more fully understand the purpose of my existence. In the hundreds of sermons that I heard in church and on the radio by men who were highly educated, he unfolded to me, without the noise of words, the real meaning of what I was hearing. I owe to this enlightening Spirit my education about the things of God; I did not get my knowledge only from books. He also gave me deep insight into human behavior, which has enabled me to help many souls oppressed by problems of sin and anguish, and the consequent discouragement. This gift of helping others was given to me because I, too, had known dreadful weakness and poverty of spirit.

Twenty years after my own conversion, I came across a passage in the Book of Ecclesiasticus (11:12, 13, 22-24) which summed up my own life:

> There is an inactive man that wants help; is very weak in ability, and full of poverty. Yet the eye of God is upon him for good, and has lifted him up from his low state and has exalted his head; and many have wondered at him, and have glorified God. . . . Trust in God, and stay in thy place. For it is easy in the eyes of God on a sudden to make the poor man rich. The blessing of God makes haste to reward the just, and in a swift hour his blessing bears fruit.

12. Love's Thrill of Joy

Irma and her mother arrived on January 15, 1944. I kissed Irma and kept my arms around her, not wanting to let her go. Her mother said, "Well, what about me?" I kissed her, too, and said, "I'm glad you came." She laughingly said, "I had no other choice. It was the only way I could get Irma off my neck!" We headed for home in a taxi, very excited and happy. I introduced them to my family and was delighted that by the time we finished supper, we were acting as if we had all known one another for years. Irma's mother had a wonderful sense of humor and, before long, I saw with great satisfaction that both our guests were very well liked by my family.

One night when we were sitting in our parlor, Irma and I had a frank discussion about the circumstances of my birth. Irma said she liked people for what they were, not for what their parents were. Her realistic and understanding attitude both relieved me and made me love her all the more.

I took Irma for a walk one evening, showing her various points of interest. As we approached St. Bernard's Church, I asked her to visit the Blessed Sacrament with me. She squeezed my hand and told me she would be very happy to. We knelt at the altar rail for a few moments, then went over to the shrine of Our Lady of Grace. While we prayed there together, I found myself whispering to her,

"I don't know how long it will be before we can be married, but I'd like to know if you will be my wife." She smiled and whispered, "Yes." I took off my military ring with its artillery crest, and slipped it on her engagement finger, saying, "I don't know if I will ever be able to give you a diamond, but the same sentiments go with this ring."

Later, I told her mother that I hoped someday to be able to go to the United States, find work, and then marry Irma. She replied, "What's wrong with getting married here and coming back with us?" I explained that I didn't feel financially able to get married right away. She had an answer for that: "My husband and I were married on a shoestring and were never sorry. The main thing is that you love each other and promise to remain faithful and face life together." She added, "I will give you the money I would have spent on a big wedding, if you are willing to settle for a small one. I am sure you will both be just as happy." She told us we would be welcome to live with her until we had a chance to get out on our own. She suggested that Irma could continue working at the watch factory and assured me it wouldn't be hard for me to get a job in Waltham.

Irma and I went to the Cathedral rectory and revealed our plans. The priest told Irma that he would write to her parish in Waltham for the necessary information and announce the banns of marriage as soon as the papers came back. I was to write to Fairville for my baptismal certificate. News of our engagement spread through the neighborhood rapidly, and my friends seemed quite happy with my choice of a wife. In our parish, marriage banns were announced from the pulpit, naming the parents of both parties; I was amused to hear that some people could hardly wait for our banns to be announced, so that after all these years they would learn who my father was! When my baptismal certificate finally arrived, we noticed it had been tampered with. In the space for the father's name was an erasure, replaced by the name of my mother's first husband. I looked at Irma in confusion and said, "What should I do?" She suggested that I take it to the pastor and let him take it from there. He apparently consulted the pastor at Fairville; when the banns were announced, the priest said only that there would be a wedding Mass on February 14 for Roy Legere and Irma Melanson.

We were married at a Mass in Assumption Cathedral. During the Holy Sacrifice, kneeling beside my wife, I could not have been happier were I being ordained a priest. Looking at Irma, I realized she had been given to me to fulfill my manhood. I would no longer be going toward God alone. I looked to the years ahead with joyful anticipation, knowing that she and I had been joined by God and were no longer two persons walking separately toward their destiny but two in one flesh, united in spirit to Jesus Christ. I heard my mother crying behind me and thought of my unknown father. I poured out prayers of petition to Jesus in the Blessed Sacrament, asking him to bless and forgive him wherever, whoever, he was.

As Irma and I received Holy Communion, a girl sang one of my favorite hymns, "Panis Angelicus," or "Bread of Angels." As a gesture of gratitude to the Blessed Virgin Mary for her role in our marriage, we also asked that an "Ave Maria" be sung. After Communion, I asked Christ to give us the grace never to violate the sacred vows of marriage by interfering with the act of procreation which made us cooperators with the Creator. I did not feel any shame or uneasiness before Christ in thinking about the pleasures awaiting me in the married state. It was a comfort to know that Christ wanted Irma and me to look upon sex with an air of wholesome joy in the Lord.

I knew enough about life to know that the path ahead of us would not be an easy one, and as we left the church I told Christ that I was relying on his generosity to give us all the help we would need in the years to come. I thanked him for sending us so many relatives and friends to witness this beautiful ceremony and to celebrate our big day with us.

On March 12, I went back to Waltham with my wife and mother-in-law. Irma went back to work, while my mother-in-law and I made the rounds to obtain the papers I needed for a permanent visa to live in Waltham. I didn't like my wife working while I did nothing. We were all disappointed to learn that I couldn't get a permanent visa without a labor exit permit from Canada. I would have to go back home to get this permit.

And so, in April, I had to say good-bye to Irma and leave by train for Canada.

13. Flaming Flashes

At Moncton, I went to the Selective Service Bureau and filed an application for the necessary permit. The manager of the office said it would take at least two weeks to get a reply from the national headquarters at Ottawa. While waiting I visited with my mother and family for a few days, then I left for Amherst, Nova Scotia, to spend two weeks with my Aunt Mary. I assisted at Mass every morning and read many books, especially the New Testament. My health was greatly improved by a daily nap and long walks around the town.

Before supper each day, I spent some time in church having heart-to-heart talks with Christ. I meditated on the enormity of my past offenses and the sufferings Christ had endured for me. I offered my separation from Irma in reparation for my sins and those of the world.

I spent many afternoons playing the accordion and singing folk songs while the elderly people at the house danced the jig. An occasional movie put the finishing touch on a well-rounded vacation and retreat.

One night, as I reached for the light cord over my bed, I looked toward the door to make sure it was closed. At that moment, I was aware that Jesus had somehow passed through the door of my room and was at the foot of my bed. My mind drank in the beauty of Christ, and I became aware of a tremendous flow of his love into my entire being. As I gazed at him standing at the foot of my bed, he flooded me with so much knowledge and instruction regarding our faith that I became fairly dizzy with the beauty and fullness of his doctrine. He opened my mind to the depth and meaning of many things in scripture that I had not fully understood.

I found myself saying, "Jesus, you are wasting your time on me. I don't even know my father's name. I am a great sinner and inconstant in your service. Why don't you give these graces to someone who will put them to good use? I know some priests, nuns and brothers who could use them better for you." I mentioned some by name; I told him about the goodness of Sister Odile, Sister Eleanor and a few others. I was referring these people to him, for he had told me that he was planning to have me do some work for him. I felt they were better qualified, and I urged him to use them instead of me. I was surprised afterwards that I hadn't told him where they lived!

I was greatly struck by his patience and politeness as he listened, smiling, to my words. His reply did not come to me through the ordinary sense of hearing but by a direct impact upon my mind. His head was tilted to one side as he said, "Roy, don't tell me what to do with my graces — I know what I'm doing." Then he asked, "Roy, do you love me?" "Yes, Lord, I do." He asked me several times to repeat my love for him. Then he asked me to love him more than I was already doing. I said to him, "I couldn't possibly love you more than I do." He said, "Will you try to love me more?" I stretched out my arms toward Christ in a gesture of love and trust as I said, "Oh, yes, Lord, I'll try, because I love you so." He seemed pleased with my words and in an instant stood at my side, filling my spirit with such an intimate love that I cannot begin to tell of the joy and peace that I experienced. Then Christ disappeared. I put out the light and lay in the darkness for several hours, trying to figure out what these visitations from Christ could be leading to. I kept this event to myself.

The next night, as I was talking about religion with Aunt Mary and some friends, I was surprised that my comments on God's love for man and his infinite mercy toward sinners moved my listeners to tears: I, an ignorant slum dweller and a novice in the practice of religion, was unexpectedly moving men's hearts. As time passed, I became convinced that Jesus had given me a gift to draw others into his merciful arms as he had drawn me. The victories of Christ over men's hearts which my unrehearsed words brought about frightened me, and his visits filled me with confusion. What did all this mean?

I left Amherst soon after, thanking Aunt Mary for a wonderful rest. I didn't tell her what had happened in her home. Two days later I heard from Ottawa: since I was only on a leave of absence from the Supply Depot, I was still in useful employment; and because of the labor shortage, my application for a visa was denied for the duration of the war. I called Irma in Waltham to tell her, and she said she would discuss the situation with her mother.

Hearing Irma's voice increased my longing to hold her in my arms and know her love again. Our separation was very trying to me; had it not been for special graces from Christ, I would not have overcome the temptations I felt on several occasions. In spite of daily Mass and Communion and visits to the Blessed Sacrament, the nights were very long, lonely and hard to bear. I begged Christ to help me persevere in the new life he had opened to me.

Many times, as I drank in the beautiful spring weather, he made his invisible presence felt and said, "Roy, you see the glorious rays of the sun, the magnificent beauty of the natural world around you. The warmth and comfort of your friends and all the true joys that this world presents to you are nothing compared to the joy that you will have in heaven if you persevere in walking in the ways of God."

When I visited him in church, he told me not to be alarmed at the trials and temptations of my present state but to remain calm and rely on his strength, especially that which I would get from receiving Holy Communion. He also instructed me to make a practice of spiritual reading.

A friend from the Reserve Army asked me to go to work for him as a clerk in his wholesale grocery business. He felt as I did, that this work would be less strenuous for me, and he offered me more money than I was getting at my other job. I decided to accept his offer. He set me up in a department of my own on the top floor of the warehouse. He told me not to push myself too hard; as long as I fulfilled certain duties putting up orders for small country stores, I was to take it easy whenever I felt the need. He had come to see me during my illness and knew it would take time for me to regain full strength. I enjoyed working in this upper room. It afforded me much solitude, which I used in thinking about God and planning a happy future for Irma and me.

In May, I got a letter from Irma and her mother, telling me to look for a small, inexpensive home. Irma's mother wanted to rent her home, bring her furniture to Canada, and live with us for the duration of the war. I found a four-room bungalow a few miles outside of Moncton, in a place called Highland View, part of

Legere's Corner where I had lived as a boy. Only a few houses in this village were finished; the rest had been thrown together and covered with tar paper and plaster. Stovepipe chimneys protruded through the roofs. This portion of Legere's Corner had only one dusty, dead-end road, with open fields along one side of it. Many of the families were on relief; others had jobs that paid very little. Most homes had several children, ill-clad and improperly fed.

I placed a down payment on a house which was to be vacated toward the end of June. (Irma had written that she wouldn't be able to come to Canada until the first week in July.) Meanwhile, when I was sitting on my long wooden bench at work, Jesus often made me aware that he was seated invisibly next to me; and when my moral struggles threatened to overwhelm me, his words of encouragement and counsel saved me from many a fall.

I became a little anxious about my mental health, because my thoughts were filled with little else than God and the things of God; and my mother warned me that if I kept going to Mass and Communion and praying so much, I would become a religious fanatic. She said I was going "religion crazy."

These thoughts did trouble me; yet, I had the presence of mind to know that my association with Christ was having just the opposite effect. My emotions were calm, and each day Christ seemed to lead me into an even greater control of my thoughts and emotions. Through his visits I learned to study his way of thinking and acting as recorded in the bible, and I found myself looking at my neighbors, their strengths and their human weaknesses, as he had done. This constant attraction of my mind and heart toward God became so strong and powerful that at the end of the day, I wondered how I had managed to get my work done and keep my boss happy with my output. He assured me he was happy with my work and hoped I would stay with him many years. Evidently the visits of Jesus and his action upon me, far from interfering with my work, were perfecting it.

There were many things which Jesus shared with me during these visits. The knowledge he imparted enabled me to help many people who crossed my path, people who wondered aloud at my ability to help them. They do not know to this day whence that help came; I felt I should keep my secret to myself, at least for the time being.

This new insight and understanding of the human weaknesses in my fellowmen (to say nothing of my own) filled me with a burning desire for the graces these people needed. I spent many hours praying for people whose names I did not know but who I realized needed help and needed it badly. Jesus taught me to include in my prayers the entire family of man. He said to me, "You may not know them, but to me, each one of them is important and I know all the circumstances of their lives."

While at work in the upper room of the warehouse, as I went down the aisles of the stockroom looking for products, I was often surprised by Jesus, who made his invisible presence known to me by what I can only call a "spiritual impression." What astonished me most of all was his hunger for love. There was no human form presented to me, that is, as if there had been a fellow worker standing there. However, my soul was convinced that the spiritual form of Christ was there somewhat after the manner of his visit to me in Amherst but now without color or features. I had always thought that God was self-sufficient, that he had no need of us or our love. That is why, when Jesus begged me to comfort him, I couldn't understand what he meant. He gave me the impression that he was embracing my spirit, caressing it with the love of God. Being new in the spiritual life, I used to try to respond to this plea for love by putting up my arms where I felt he was standing, going through the motion of putting my arms around him. This was the only way I knew of to satisfy the yearnings of Christ for comfort from me.

I now know that these associations with Christ were interior encounters; my bodily senses were left completely untouched. Jesus gave me the impression that my love was a comfort to him, but I didn't know why. He came to me in this same manner even during an occasional movie, seeking comfort, so it seemed to me, in the midst of great agony.

Frequently, as I knelt at the Communion rail, he would make me aware of his yearning to be united to the children of men. This eagerness in the heart of the Savior surprised me, overwhelmed me. Sometimes during these spiritual conversations with our Lord, I lamented the fact that I had so many faults; he told me he was not too concerned with my failings, but rather was pleased with my daily efforts to overcome them.

I asked many friends about their spiritual lives, to see if any of them would describe their experiences as I have attempted to describe mine. Finding none whose lives resembled mine, I began again to fear for my mental health. Several times in confession, I asked different priests if I might tell them about my spiritual life. They would always encourage me to speak; but no matter how hard I tried to explain what was going on in my soul, I couldn't express

myself to any of them. The only thing that kept me going was the
fact that these visits from Christ seemed to me to be God's doing;
where else could they have come from?

My association with Christ naturally brought me great joy.
And strangely enough, it heightened my enjoyment of recreation
such as bowling, movie-going, listening to music and dancing. At
times, however, Christ drew me away from such things, urging me
to leave the company of my friends to converse with him about the
spiritual welfare of the world of men.

I could not make these visits of Christ take place no matter
how much I longed for him. His coming was always unexpected;
and when he did come, I could not have fled from him had I wished
to. Many times I made up my mind that I would ignore him if he
ever presented himself to me again — not because I mistrusted him,
but because I wanted a spiritual path which would be less bewildering,
the path several of my friends were following in great peace of
mind. I almost envied the way they advanced toward heaven, content to do good and avoid evil. But Christ kept urging me on to
greater effort, greater love and greater perfection; and I didn't
know how far he wanted me to go. As hard as I tried, he demanded
more and more of me.

One night, after bowling with a friend, I returned home, got
into bed, and lit a cigarette. As I put the match into the ash tray,
I glanced, then stared, at the statue of the Sacred Heart of Jesus in
my room. The face of the statue seemed to come alive and the
eyes of Jesus held mine in a magnetic gaze. His piercing eyes shed
a ray of burning love which seemed to burn the very center of
my heart. I was aware of being seized and held, a willing captive,
by the fire of his eternal love. Had he not sustained my weak human
nature, I would certainly have died of joy that night.

When I calmed down, I asked Jesus what he wanted of me. I
knelt on the floor and heard him say, "Roy, I want your heart,
and I want you to make known that I thirst for the hearts of your
fellowmen. Tell them of my love; tell them how much I love them
and how eager is my desire to see them loving God their Father in
time and in eternity." He let me see in his gaze the awesome depth
of his love for all mankind which had led him to become one of us
and suffer and die for our salvation. He made me aware of the
great need for men to love and serve God by fulfilling the commandments in their everyday living. He made known to me his
desire that I should use every opportunity to draw souls to him. I
was given to understand that I was to do this by speaking about his

love and putting to use the knowledge that he had so freely given me; the graces and favors he had given me were not meant for me alone. I understood that my heart was no longer my own but belonged to him, and that he was going to awaken in me the desire to reach others with this message of love. He told me he would assist me in my efforts. When he left me, I crept into bed quietly and slept very little that night.

When I came home for lunch the next day, I sat on the couch looking at the statue, recalling the event of the night before and the many extraordinary experiences of the past several months. The statue now appeared as it had always been in our home — a plaster replica of what some artist felt Christ might have looked like. I was having an after-dinner cigarette when, suddenly, the face came to life again. This time, a glorious light emanated from the face of Christ, then his image seemed to recede into this ray of light and I saw the image of my own face in its place. My face bore the marks of old age and my hair was white as snow. As I looked at this mysterious scene, I saw my face fade into the strange light and the living face of Jesus reappear, then immediately disappear.

Some years later, I spoke to a priest about this, explaining how the face of Christ had dissolved into mine. He told me he felt that this strange phenomenon symbolized the effect of Baptism by which I became incorporated into the living Christ; and I was meant to be one with him in time and in eternity. He told me that in the bible eternity is sometimes symbolized by white hair. For my part, I believed that Christ used this statue or image of his sacred humanity to reflect the marvel of his spiritual encounter with my soul. I think he gave me this help because I was not spiritually advanced enough to understand what was taking place between him and my spirit, and I needed this visible sign to enlighten me.

14. Probing Old Wounds

In June, 1944, Irma wrote to tell me that she was expecting our first child and would come to Canada in a few weeks. She and her mother arrived in Moncton on July 1. At last, in our new home, we had the privacy we longed for.

During this time, we had several discussions about my unknown father. Irma felt I should make an attempt to find out who he was. She said it was important for us to know so that we might be sure, at least to the best of our ability, that our children might not be led by chance into marrying their blood relatives. I, too, wanted to settle the matter of my parentage. When tempted to give up my struggles in the spiritual life, I received many inner suggestions which I felt were coming from the devil — although some of them may have come from my own imagination playing on my fears. It seemed that the devil whispered to me that evil tendencies were in my blood and would run in the blood of my children, and neither I nor they would ever be able to rise above this to please God. This troubled me very much and I asked my Lord to help me overcome these fears and persevere in his love and service. Still, I was reluctant to ask my mother who my father was, afraid of hurting her feelings by talking about so delicate a subject.

I went many times to ask her, but lost my nerve because my appreciation of the sacredness of marriage made my birth seem to me even worse. The more I thought about it, the more I realized that I *must* find out, at least for the sake of my children. One night, finding my mother alone, I said, "Mom, now that I am married, I feel you should tell me," and I gave her my reasons. She began to cry. I felt a surge of rebellion rise in me as she said, "It's none of your business." I tried to keep calm as I told her I had the right to know. I explained some of the deep sufferings that the circumstances of my birth had caused me. She said, "No one will ever know!" and then told me that even Beatrice and Fidele had never been told. I put my arms around her before I left and asked her to reflect on what I had said. Then I went home.

That night, Irma asked how things had gone during the visit to my mother. I tried to explain, but my voice broke and I couldn't go on. She held me close in her arms. I thanked God that the child she was carrying would never have to know sorrows like its father's. I offered the grief in my heart to Jesus Christ to do with what he would, and fell asleep.

I stopped in at my mother's one day after work, and she told me she would write for my birth certificate. A couple of weeks later, during another visit, she called me upstairs where we would be alone. As I followed her into the bedroom, I prayed for the strength I would need for this very decisive moment. My mother handed me the birth certificate in silence. I unfolded it and read it. It was an official certificate of birth from the Provincial Government, and did not read "father unknown," as had some other documents I had seen, but had on it the name of the man in question. I asked my mother, "Were you married at the time?" She said, "No, but I didn't know any better, so I told the doctor this man's name and he just filled it in like routine business." I then wondered aloud if my father or perhaps my half brothers or sisters were not too far away from Moncton. My mother dispelled this notion, telling me that he was a citizen of the United States. She had known him for some time in New Brunswick. She believed him to be dead.

She told me that I looked like my father — I was about the same build and had many of his mannerisms. She told me he was a good man and also very intelligent. I said to her, "Mom, things must have been very hard for you." She started to cry as she told me of the many hardships she had endured at the hands of her relatives. I put my arms around her and kissed her, telling her that I loved her very much. She smiled at me through her tears, very grateful for these words. I said to her, "This is a French name but very unlike most of the French-Canadian names that we know."

She explained that my grandparents had emigrated from France. As I held the document in my hands I felt a little better. I had established at least the beginnings of my self-identity. My mother didn't want to go into detail concerning my father or explain why they weren't married, so I thanked her and slipped quietly out of the house.

I knew I would have to do something about this paper; it was the only legal record of my birth, and all my other papers — school records, marriage certificate, service records, etc. — were made out in the name of Legere. One day, Irma and I took the paper to a lawyer and explained the situation to him. He told me he would save me the embarrassment of appearing in court and would see that all was taken care of according to my wishes. When I was called back to his office, he handed me a birth certificate, which read: "Joseph Roy, son of Sylvia Legere," and "Father Unknown." The lawyer explained that I was now able to use the Legere name legally. The burden, at long last, had been lifted.

I also wanted to know how I was registered in the books of the church at the time of my Baptism. My mother-in-law and I took a train to St. John and a bus from there to the parish church in Fairville. I don't remember the pastor's name; but from the moment he greeted us, he was very kind. I told him who I was and what I was looking for. He went to a large safe, pulled out a record book marked "1922 — Baptisms," and began thumbing through the pages. He said, "Yes, here you are," and called me over to his side. I looked at the entry: "Baby boy baptized — Joseph Roy." It had nothing where the parents' names should have been entered. Under my two names were the names, "George Wallace and Mary LeBlanc, godparents." Seeing I was troubled, he said, "Actually, it's no one's fault. We do not know any of the circumstances or motivations on the part of either party. It is best to leave this to almighty God, who is goodness itself. I have some idea of what you are going through. You are one of many, many thousands, Roy, so don't feel too badly about it." I told him, "I used to think that the Church hated us." He then told me that St. Pius X, realizing how much like martyrs illegitimate children can be, wished he could canonize all of them. We thanked the priest for his kindness and left.

As we were walking down the street toward the bus stop, Irma's mother said, "Roy, when you looked at that entry, you turned white. I thought you were going to drop to the floor." I looked at her and replied, with as much of a smile as I could muster, "That makes two of us!"

At times, I felt a great urge to find my father. I talked this over with my wife, who advised me, "I don't think it would be wise for you to find him and make yourself known to him — perhaps he is still alive and happily married with children, and I don't think you would want to be responsible for hurting any of these people." This made great sense to me and I agreed to leave well enough alone. There came a time, however, when my resolve weakened.

Irma and I were in another town and heard that someone with the same name as my father lived nearby. One night I talked Irma into going to a phone booth with me to look for names corresponding to the one on my birth certificate. I found one whose first name was an abbreviated form of my father's; I dialed the number. A young man about my age answered, and I explained that I was looking for someone with his name who would probably be around 55. "That fits my father's description and age, but he is buried here in town." I asked him if he had any brothers and sisters and he said he did. He wanted to know if there was anything he could do for me. I told him I might call again.

I was excited about the idea of meeting my half brothers and sisters, and expressed this desire to Irma. She took me by the hand and led me from the phone booth. We walked for some time through the streets, just talking. She again reminded me that I might unintentionally hurt others if I persisted. She said, "Let's concentrate on you and me and our own little family and do what we can to have a happy married life and raise our children to be good." I knew she was right.

15. Joy -- From Within and Without

Irma wrote to her sister, Dora, in Fitchburg, Massachusetts, to arrange to stay with her so that our first child could be born an American citizen. I knew I was going to miss Irma, but I felt this was the best thing to do; we hoped the war would end soon and we would be able to settle in that country which was so dear to both of us.

At work one day, I was in a secluded area of the warehouse in search of some item when I was suddenly stunned by an overpowering sense of the presence of the Blessed Trinity. I had always believed God was everywhere; I learned this in parochial school and accepted it without being affected by it. But this new experience brought me to my knees. In a shadowy corner of the warehouse that afternoon there was nothing visible to the human eye; with the "eye of my soul" I became aware of the presence of three Persons in one God. This strange event was similar to my experience on the country road in LeBlanc Office except that, then, the "presence" seemed to be the power of God over nature. This was something more.

The idea of three Persons in one God had always baffled me. But as I knelt there my understanding was satisfied; what I had only believed I now "saw." Joy and love filled my spirit; I knew I was being loved by the three Divine Persons. This majestic presence of God not only humbled me but filled me with peace such as I had never read about or experienced before. All the religious experiences of my life up to this point seemed as nothing compared to this unexpected meeting with the Godhead. This experimental knowledge of God near me, loving me, did more to increase my faith in his love for me and in his other attributes than years of study could have accomplished. I was so convinced of the presence of the three Persons in God that I would have died rather than deny this particular visit by almighty God. My intellect became aware of the tremendous, glorious majesty of God and it was given to me to understand the awesome chasm between the power and beauty of God and myself, a mere creature. I prostrated full length, face down in the dust on the warehouse floor.

I found myself adoring and praising the Father and then in turn his Eternal Son and the Holy Spirit; then I again adored them in the Triune Godhead. I longed for the day of eternal existence in heaven when all my human blindness would be removed so I could sing out to God's family how good and merciful he had been to me while I walked this earth. This favor from God gave me a vast new insight into the spotless purity of God, a purity I must aspire to if I would become a worthy bearer of God in my body.

This experience was repeated on several occasions. In one of these visitations, the Holy Trinity made my mind aware that the three of them were living in me, in the center of my soul. This revelation was so illuminating and comforting that I thought I would faint from sheer happiness. I adored these three Persons of God in me with fervor, telling them I loved them and was truly grateful for their astonishing kindness. Now I knew what Jesus meant when he told us in the gospels that if we keep his commandments, the Divine Trinity will come and abide in us. I was more determined than ever to receive Christ in Holy Communion so that this life of God in me would increase and completely possess my soul. I now understood the meaning of the scriptural passage: "He is not far from each of us, for in him we live and breathe and are." This encounter with my Creator made me realize how much of a nothing I would be without him.

I asked some of my friends if they had ever heard of such an experience, and they shook their heads. I became worried again about my mental health; was my imagination, my mind, betraying me? I asked a priest, after explaining this experience to him, if it was lawful to genuflect in adoration of this presence of God; he said it was. The idea of loving God and wanting to love him more filled my mind almost constantly. I wanted to die and to be with God forever.

I don't know how my friends and relatives saw a change in me, but it soon became apparent that they did. One day a cousin said to me, "Roy, someone asked the other day if I had noticed a strange look in your eyes. What's the matter?" I didn't know what to say. I was troubled in my inability to explain the activities of my soul to a priest or anyone else. Whenever I tried, I only fumbled for words. At times, I thought perhaps I had become what some had feared, "religion crazy." I tried many times to explain myself to Irma, but my lips were sealed. I had the feeling of being a stranger to my family and friends. I met a young man named Alderic in the Third Order. He was a good companion, a very religious person with both feet on the ground. I questioned him several times about his prayer life and he told me that he knew nothing of what I had experienced. This made me wonder even more if I weren't losing my mind; he obviously loved God very much but was walking along a different path altogether.

My new association with God made me homesick for heaven. I felt like an exile in a strange country. I knew that the people around me were good; but compared to the divine presence I felt within me, they seemed as nothing and I had to exert the greatest effort to keep interested in anything that wasn't God. This is very hard to describe; but that is the way it was. Still, I applied myself to all my duties even more diligently than before, because I knew it was the will of God. This experience of the presence of God in me led to greater self-denial and more study and thought about spiritual realities. I noticed that now I was serving God more out of love than fear of eternal punishment, a welcome change.

At times during prayer I couldn't find words to express my love for God; so I simply said, "O my God, I love you!" or "My God and my all!" My awareness of God within me gave me new strength to live my life in Christ. I knew I did not have to be afraid of the special favors God had given me; I was sure that if I just listened to his Church and followed his commandments I would have nothing to fear.

On December 7, 1944, Irma left for Fitchburg to give birth to our first baby. When Christmas came, my mother-in-law and I went to Amherst to spend the holidays with Aunt Mary. She was very good to us and made Irma's absence a little easier to take. Three days after Christmas, while working at the warehouse, I received a telegram from my wife; I was the father of a daughter.

I sent Irma a telegram thanking her for our baby girl and asking God's blessing on them both.

I again applied for a labor exit permit, explaining that my wife and daughter were American citizens now in the United States, and that I hoped to be allowed to join them. In January it was refused; I would have to wait until the war ended. I wrote to Irma, and she made plans to come home. She arrived by train with our child, Sharon Anne, on February 12, 1945. Sharon was six weeks old when I first held her in my arms at the station.

Once Irma had adjusted to caring for Sharon, her mother went back to the States to live with Irma's sister, Edith, and her husband, Tony. This gave Irma and me the new experience of living alone. We were a happy family. We both liked classical music and spent many evenings holding hands, listening to the radio and admiring our baby. It was a great joy to hold my baby in my arms and feel her smooth soft cheek next to mine. Many times while feeling the pride of being a father, the haunting desire to know my own father would rise up inside me. During one of my visits to Christ in the Blessed Sacrament, I asked him to help me overcome this urge to seek out my father. Jesus let me hear him speaking by means of an inner voice; to my amazement, he repeated the words he had spoken to me when I was 17: "Roy, my Father wants you to be his son." He went on, "You are important to him and to me, for by Baptism you have been born again and you are now truly the son of the Father of Fathers, in reality the only real Father there is, for all other fathers receive their fatherhood from him." He showed me the honorable and noble aspect of human fatherhood, even as he explained to my mind the precedence of the Fatherhood of God.

These words of Christ and others that he impressed on my mind made me understand for the first time the essence of the doctrine of Baptism. I knew so little about the doctrines of my faith! He reminded me of what he had said to Nicodemus: "Unless a man be born again of water and the spirit, he cannot enter the kingdom of heaven." He explained to me that in Baptism I became incorporated into himself, and showed me how I had become God's adopted son, sharing in the very nature of God. Jesus explained to me that, in the family of God, he is not only my redeemer but my big brother, since he was the firstborn of God's sons.

This knowledge began to ease greatly the pain of the story of my birth. Jesus gently closed the wound in my heart, and today there is no longer a scar — just a fleeting memory now and then to remind me of my spiritual dignity, which springs from sharing in God's divine nature and the splendor of my eternal destiny. He said, "Roy, as the Father has loved me, so I have loved you." Jesus unfolded to me the divine logic and wisdom of God's plan for man's divine adoption. And in this plan I saw the emptiness of material things.

He told me why my second birth was more important than my first: "In the first you were born of man and of blood. But in your second birth, a recreation in me, you are born of God through water and the power of the Holy Spirit." He made me understand that I belonged to the most wonderful family there is — the divine family of God. He also made it known that I have unnumbered brothers and sisters in Christ. He said I was of greater worth in the eyes of God than royalty in the family of man: "Since God is king and ruler of all creation and you are now his son, you are in reality, Roy, a prince in the kingdom of God." In making me realize my true worth as a child of God, Christ gave me a lasting peace of mind and soul. All the joys I have ever known in my natural life and in my spiritual life were climaxed in one striking incident a few days after Christ had taught me how I had become a son of God and what this meant.

I was returning to work from lunch, and was about halfway up the stairs to my department in the warehouse. I had taken my arm out of one sleeve of my jacket, when I was suddenly stopped by the sight of Christ standing at the head of the stairs. He said, "Roy, I have been waiting for you." I was aware that he was embracing my spirit as a divine Friend and big Brother in God, an embrace which filled me with a reverent, grateful, humble love for God. He continued, "Roy, I want you to meet your Father and mine." I knew immediately that he was about to present me to his heavenly Father, and I cannot describe the anticipation and joy that filled my spirit. I was greatly impressed by the politeness of Christ, who could have said, "My Father and yours" instead of "your Father and mine." In this experience, he seemed to lead me to the center of the room in which I worked, and then I heard him say, "Eternal Father, here is one of your other sons." It is impossible for me to describe this encounter with God the Father, for there are just no words I can use to express what happened. My spirit was made aware of a great eagerness on the part of our heavenly Father to welcome me. This eternal God clasped me to his bosom and with a great surge of love and tenderness, called out to me, "My son, my son, my son!" I cried out from the depths of my soul, "O my God, O my Father!"

I felt at home with the Blessed Trinity, for I shared their divine nature through Baptism and the merits of Jesus Christ. I was made to realize that the paternal love and solicitude which God was expressing for me were typical of his loving concern for all his adopted children. I can only stammer in my attempt to speak of the joy I felt at finding out how much he loves his dear family of man. I got the impression that Jesus received much pleasure and satisfaction in presenting any soul of good will to his Father; that, as a member of this family of God, I was receiving love from the Father, and the elder Son, Christ, and the Holy Spirit, the eternal source of love, who seemed to unite all of us with a great strength and power — made known to me through the symbol of a million roaring hurricanes. During this experience, Jesus flashed before my mind many quotations from Sacred Scripture, describing our adoption as sons of God. Many of these texts I had never before understood; but as each one passed before my mind, he clarified for me the truth and depth of these sacred utterances.

This experience also gave me a greater understanding of God's purpose in the creation of man. I marveled at the ingenuity of the mind of God in planning such wonderful gifts for his creatures. At times, I could hardly wait for the time when I would leave this world and go back to him from whom I had received my existence. At other times, I found myself wishing that I didn't have to work, so I could go from town to town and tell everyone about the wonderful destiny to which they are called. But God's will seemed to be that I should go on as I was, working, keeping his commandments and listening to his Church. Jesus never tired of repeating that as long as I would follow the Church he had left to teach, guide and sanctify, I need never fear losing my way.

Another thing this experience did for me was to remove all fear of death and of the unknown world beyond the grave. Now I knew in part what was waiting for those who sincerely try their best to know, love and serve God and to love their neighbor for his sake. In fact, I found myself almost envying those who were going into eternity ahead of me.

Having learned that the Blessed Trinity abides in the deepest recesses of the human soul, I formed the habit of adoring God in others, realizing they were also living tabernacles of the Most High. When my obligations did not permit me to visit Christ in the Blessed Eucharist, I adored him in other people. Not only did I feel this was giving glory to God, but it also proved to be a great boon in my struggle to preserve chastity. Although I was spiritually enlightened, I was not blind to the comeliness of a feminine form, and many and varied were my temptations. Full of the virility and passion of youth, I was grateful to God many times for helping me preserve my soul in a state of grace. The presence of God in others became my main reason for not violating these holy temples by carrying out the desires that rose up inside me.

The crafty angel of hell tried to persuade me to give up the practice of adoring God in others by telling me, "For all you know, *I* may be in these very people. They could well be my agents." I remember telling him that this could be true but, even so, I could still adore God in them, for he is present by his sustaining power, without which they would cease to exist. This awakening to the presence of God in myself and in others opened up new horizons in the spiritual world and made my life a wonderful adventure.

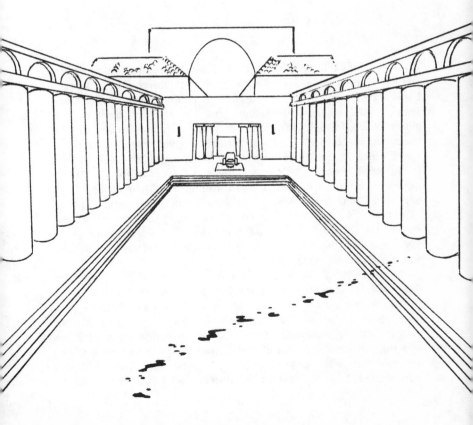

16. Pain and Union

One night during Lent of 1945, Jesus showed me his power in one of my dreams. I was taken in spirit back to the time of Christ. I was standing in the palace courtyard of Pontius Pilate. I remember distinctly the magnificent building and the rows of giant marble pillars which formed long corridors leading from the courtyard to the main palace building. I was surprised to find myself standing in blood which had fallen in large drops. I felt numb as I noticed tiny fragments of human flesh in and near the drops of blood. While gazing at this strange sight, I heard a thunderous roar coming from one of the corridors. People were shouting and screaming, "Crucify him, crucify him!" I asked some stranger what the commotion was about. He answered, "They are going to crucify Jesus of Nazareth. He has already been here once," he said, as he pointed to the flesh and blood on the stone courtyard.

Great crowds began to assemble where I stood. They were filled with gleeful anticipation. When I realized that I was about to witness Jesus on his way to Calvary to die for me, I nearly died from remorse for my thousands of sins which had offended this eternal Lover of mankind. Great sorrow oppressed me as, for the first time in my life, the full significance of the awful price Christ paid for our souls sank deep into my mind and heart. My ears were deafened by the roar of the throng, and I pushed my way to the front of the crowd so I could see Jesus pass by. As I stood waiting for him, I thought, "Oh, how I would like to speak to him and tell him how sorry I am for the burden my sins have laid upon him!" I knew I could never get close to him, but I also realized he was God and would be able to read my heart. This thought comforted me a little, as I wanted Jesus to know that someone was sorry for all his sufferings.

As he and his tormentors drew near, the noise grew frightful and I thought all hell had broken loose. I saw him bent over by the weight of the cross, blood streaming from his body. As I whispered, "O Jesus, I am sorry; please help me to follow you by leading a good life," the Savior turned to his left and walked toward me. The crown of thorns was pressed deeply within his brow and his face was covered with blood. He carried the cross on his left shoulder. As he came to me, he put his right arm around my neck. With his bleeding face pressed against mine, our Lord made me aware that my sorrow for my sins and concern for him in his agony had brought him much comfort, and that he was embracing me to show his gratitude. I understood that his embrace was a symbol of an invitation extended to me. My mind distinctly heard the unspoken words, "I want you to reach perfect union with me."

He made me understand that Christian marriage was a symbol of what he hoped to accomplish in my spiritual life. I asked myself, "Is there such a thing as spiritual marriage?" He fixed a loving gaze on me; and as I returned his look of love, I saw in his eyes the eternal glory of his divine nature. At the same time, I realized the precious value of the human soul as understood by Jesus Christ, who longed to save every last one from eternal torment in hell. The full significance of Christ's mission was burnt into my mind and memory forever. I stood there transfixed, as it were, by the magnetic power of love. In all that I saw and heard in this dream it was above all else the loving gaze of Jesus that pierced my soul and left in it a degree of love unknown to me before.

I was greatly moved to compassion for Jesus as I saw the deep sadness in his look; in spite of his intense love and suffering many unfortunate souls would deliberately choose the path to hell and so separate themselves forever from his loving embrace. The guards, who had now recovered from their surprise at what he was doing, grabbed him and pulled him away from me, saying brutally, "Come on, come on."

When I recovered from this startling and unexpected embrace of the Son of God made man, I turned to leave. Then I noticed about 20 babies lying on the ground. They were wrapped up in winding strips of cloth, after the ancient Jewish custom. I asked, "Why are they on the ground?" A mysterious voice made it known that I was looking at some of the Holy Innocents, then said to me, "You, too, will suffer their fate because of what Christ just did and said to you." I wondered at the time if someone in our century would be called upon to suffer death at the point of a sword for the cause of Christ; then I realized that these words could be a prediction that I was to undergo a martyr's fate.

As the dream continued, I saw myself back in the 20th century, walking the streets to my home. I said, "What can this mean? No one will believe me when I tell them what happened to me." As I walked toward the house, I was resolved and determined to arouse my family and the whole world to a realization of God's love for mankind which had led the Father to send his only-begotten Son to redeem us from the powers of hell through the sufferings of the crucifixion.

Upon awakening, I began a new period in my life, marked by a sharp insight into our ungratefulness toward God and the great hunger of Christ for souls. For several days I kept this strange event locked in my heart. One night, confused and bewildered, I decided to talk it over with Irma, who was surprised and said, "I have always thought that the value of such dreams ended with the apostles." I could not bring myself to agree with her because this was another link in the mysterious dreams and visions which were drawing my soul closer and closer to God. Still afraid I was losing my sanity, I attempted to shake off these disturbing occurrences as delusions of my imagination. But as Christ began to form the definite pattern of an appeal for love, I found myself falling into a sort of psychological spell which I was powerless to shake off. The vision of the bleeding Christ and his words to me are indelible in my soul. I believe they will remain there for all eternity.

The recollection of this dream has sustained me whenever my life has been flooded with temptations against faith, hope and love. It has also created a longing to spend my remaining years working to draw all the souls I possibly can to share in the plentiful redemption wrought for us by Christ. I was so disturbed by this experience that I decided to talk it over with a priest who was trained and qualified to help me understand it. I chose a doctor of theology. In the confessional one night I asked him, "Father, does God come to anyone in dreams in this day and age?" "Yes, he does, but the Church must be very cautious in these matters. Why do you ask?"

I told him about the dream of Christ's passion. He asked, "Are you a married man?" "Yes, Father, I am. I guess I had better try to forget the whole thing." "My son," he said, "I want you to remember what Jesus said to you but don't elaborate on it." I was still very confused, but I knew I was walking a safe path as long as I listened to the Church and her priests, for Christ had said to his first bishops and priests, "Lo, I am with you all days, even to the consummation of the world. He who hears you hears me."

The words of Christ haunted me day and night. I had been taught as a boy that Christ was the "Bridegroom of the soul," but I never understood it. I wondered what Jesus could have meant by marriage as a symbol of spiritual union with him. I also tried to picture what else he wanted to tell me when they pulled him away. One day I picked up a little pamphlet in church and stuck it in my pocket for further reading. Traveling back and forth to work by bus gave me a good chance to study the faith in little doses. On one such trip I reached into my work jacket and pulled out the leaflet I had bought. As I opened it at random, my eyes caught a glimpse of two words: "mystical marriage." It was the word "marriage" connected with religion that aroused my curiosity, and I immediately thought of Christ asking me for full union with him. This is what the paragraph said: "Mystical marriage of the soul with Christ in a union of love is the highest state of perfection or holiness that a soul can reach on this earth." My hair almost stood on end as the meaning of Christ's words sank into my mind and soul. Jesus had actually asked me to become a saint, to unite my soul to him by blending my life and will with his. The booklet quoted St. Paul's words to the Thessalonians (4:3): "You are called to be saints, for this is the will of God, your sanctification."

As I read further, I learned that there are many degrees of holiness among the followers of Christ, but none is higher than that attained in the mystical marriage of the soul with Christ, the Savior of mankind. I gradually came to realize that I was not a victim of the devil's tricks or foolish thinking on my own part; the visions and strange dreams had, after all, drawn me closer to Jesus and to a better life. They either introduced me to or confirmed the teachings of the Church and Sacred Scripture. I did not know why Christ chose one so low, stupid and weak; but I knew that he had won my heart and I was determined to follow this strange path unafraid, for I had his Church to guide my footsteps and keep me from defeating his plans through ignorance.

One day I asked a priest if the words of St. Paul to the Thessalonians were also meant for me, and he said they were. I didn't know how to become a saint. I asked a good Christian woman, and she replied, "A saint is one who does everything he can to follow the will of God as he makes it known through his laws, the teachings of Christ, and the circumstances of his divine providence." That, then, would be my goal — to follow the will of God. I knew what his will was, in part; for the rest, I would wait and see.

Once Christ had mysteriously manifested his sacred Passion to me and urged me to closer union with him through the perfect fulfillment of his will, I was determined to accept his invitation and follow him at all costs. But I needed more knowledge and guidance along the ways of the world of grace, still so new to me, and so confusing. Knowing that the bible contains the wisdom of God, I began to read it frequently, in the hope that I might discover in scripture the principles needed to guide and direct my steps. At first, I found these writings extremely difficult. I was not used to thinking or understanding complicated plans, and the bible did seem complicated. I used to wish I could "boil down" all its laws and principles to one simple idea within the grasp of my limited understanding.

Knowing my thoughts, Christ came to my aid. One day as I was protesting to him that I had a simple mind and little education and that I needed special help if I was ever to understand his ways, he opened my mind by saying to me in a secret manner, "Roy, do you remember how I gave you what I call a 'shortcut' to me? I explained to you how to love me with your whole mind and heart and strength and soul, and your neighbor for love of me." I told him I remembered. He then made me aware that in keeping the great commandment of love, I was already learning the deepest secret of the spiritual life and progressing along its ways. He instructed me that I was to discover his will by always remembering the commandment of love, and by keeping myself alert to what he expected of me in all the circumstances of life, one day at a time. He said that he would help me to discover his will in these circumstances and that I must often think of the example of love he had shown in his own life.

Our Lord then recalled to my mind how he had called me a prince in the kingdom of God. He made me realize that every loyal prince will show his love for his king in a practical way and go further by extending his love toward all other subjects of the king. True nobility, he reminded me, brings with it certain obligations — *noblesse oblige.* Because I was nobly born as a son of the great

King, I must be sure that my way of living was truly noble and my conduct befitting of a child of the royal family of God. He left me with these words, "To help you understand how you are to act in every circumstance of life, stop and think how I have loved you and how I have expressed my love for you." My life, henceforth, was to be ruled by love, love like that of Christ.

This led me to reread the life of Christ in the gospels. I was determined to know more about him. As I read, he was by my side, helping me to understand the meaning of many details of his life, things I could never have understood otherwise. I found myself more and more eager for solitude where I could think upon these things and quietly adore my God and my all. I was happy to recognize that I was leading a hidden life, unknown to others, just as the Master had lived it.

The Passion of Christ seemed to hold a special message for me. I knew I wasn't expected to be nailed to a material cross as he was, but I could imitate him by a secret crucifixion of my inner self, of my selfishness and vanity, and by fighting against my undisciplined passions. I soon found out what the scriptural phrase "crucify the old man" meant in me. Though I was aware that the Son of God was filling me with strength to conquer the base inclinations of my nature, the remnants of original sin, I was not free from struggle. My poor human nature balked, kicked, squirmed and rebelled against the effort of the Spirit. The "natural man," so much alive in me, complained and fought for survival like a mad dog. It screamed, "If I submit to the Spirit, I will no longer be free!" This became a dreadful fear. Was I to lose my freedom?

It wasn't too long before I learned what it was to be *really* free. After so many years of fighting against my weak human nature, Christ liberated me in a striking manner. I found myself possessed of a new kind of freedom, a freedom born of the knowledge that God had established a harmony between my body and my spirit. I saw that my will had been given its rightful place in governing my actions. My emotions no longer had the power to rule over my reason or influence it unduly. I seemed to know what I have read about so many times as the ideal of all human striving, the meaning of integrity — "wholeness" — in a man. What a great sense of strength and power to find this "right order" restored to the soul! I really felt I had become a "he-man" in the eyes of God. I felt more the conqueror than worldly generals and rulers who had conquered entire nations. This new sense of self-discipline and self-mastery was the most exciting victory of my life.

But it was not a final victory! Precisely because of the new strength I felt within me, I fell into a trap. I became complacent. I did the one thing which is the greatest pitfall of life: I let down my guard. Because of this, I became the victim of surprise attacks of sin. Then, ashamed of myself, I would go weeping to Christ, kneeling at the back of the church to signify my unworthiness to appear before him. One day he addressed my intellect and said, "Roy, I allowed this to happen to you to show you that you are totally dependent on me and to remind you that without me you can do nothing." This is a hard, cold lesson to learn.

Jesus made me aware that the struggle against the enemies of my soul would go on until I drew my last breath. I would never be free of the struggle of being a man. He told me, however, not to become disheartened but to remember that his words, "Watch and pray," hold a very deep meaning, and I must learn to apply them to my life. I expressed my sorrow to him, and he urged me to use the sacrament of Penance frequently, even when there were no serious sins to confess. This sacrament would give me greater strength to overcome the habits of my past sinful life. To help in my struggle against sin, I began practicing physical mortifications — until one day Jesus made it known to me that these are good and useful but not meant for me. My health had not been vigorous since my long periods of sickness. He asked me to discontinue the severe penances and to apply myself more to concentrating my thoughts upon him and relying totally on him. He indicated that he would be satisfied if I continued my sincere efforts to follow the instructions he had given me so often in the past. These directives of Christ were confirmed for me one night by a priest adviser who refused to let me practice bodily penances of an irritating nature, telling me that if I applied myself to living the commandments and fulfilling the duties of my state in life, I would be taking care of all the penance I could handle. This confirmation of my interior life by a directive from a priest was once again a sure pathway to follow.

17. Little Friends of Christ

In his many visits, Christ made me aware that he wanted me to show others the same loving concern he had shown me. I longed to see people receive the freedom which his truth would bring them and to have them enjoy the peace which results from harmony with his holy will. I had often taken advantage of isolated opportunities by speaking of God's love, but had not as yet done anything on a large scale to bring souls to God. The opportunity was soon to come.

One afternoon in May, 1945, I looked out the window and noticed a boy of about 12 playing in the street near my front yard. I was attracted by the look of loneliness on his face. I recognized him as a boy who lived a few houses down the street. Then I realized why he looked so alone and unhappy — like myself, he had suffered abuse from the neighbors and their children because of the circumstances of his birth. I saw in him a reflection of my own sad boyhood. I called to the lad and asked him to come in. He smiled and ran toward me. Irma and I welcomed him and gave him some lunch. Afterwards, we asked him to join us in the family rosary. I used meditations to suit his young mind. I saw I was reaching him as I dwelt on God's love, especially for the poor and lonely. I mentioned our Lord's desire to lead all without exception to heaven. After we had prayed, we spent some time talking with the boy and encouraging him. The next evening, I answered a knock at my door, and to my surprise there stood my new young

friend with 15 other youngsters, some in rags. They promptly informed me they had come to say the rosary. Two of them held up
old rosaries to convince me. We welcomed them, dirt, rags and all.
I led them in prayer, with appropriate meditations. We gave them
some candy before they left and told them they were welcome anytime.

Nothing happens by chance; I was convinced that God's loving
providence was sending these youngsters night after night. One
evening, two weeks after my first guest had arrived, our little bungalow
was filled to capacity. After prayers, I went to the door to say
"Good-night" and saw my lawn covered with children still on their
knees! Unknown to me, they had been praying with all of us inside
the house. One woman, seeing a gang of kids kneeling in front of
my house, hurried to telephone our pastor. He sent word to bring
the children to an abandoned boardinghouse a few doors down
from our place, which belonged to the parish. It had been converted
into two classrooms where some Sisters of Notre Dame had tried
to lift these children out of their ignorance; they finally had to give
up. The first night we held our "mission" services, 98 of my little
friends came to our new meeting place. During one of his precious
visits, Christ had said, "Roy, someday you will do great things for
me"; I wondered if this was the beginning. My friend Alderic, from
the Third Order, offered to help me with the youngsters. We planned
a campaign of instruction, for the children had been throwing questions at me: "Does God really love me? . . . Does he like the poor?
. . . Will he help me?"

We met at the little mission every night after work, and for
an hour and a half I would talk about their real importance in the
eyes of God. I used the same technique Jesus had used with me,
without revealing my private spiritual life. Alderic and I split the
group in two — 45 who had received First Communion and 53
ranging in age from four to seven. Many knew nothing at all about
praying. Several in the older group hadn't been to Communion in
years. They all had something in common: they were looking for
love, knowledge of God, and assurance they could go to heaven.
I played the accordion while we sang hymns and folk songs. They
accompanied me by clapping and tapping their feet. We set up a
little shrine to the Holy Family and the youngsters roamed the fields,
picking flowers for it. Some of the mothers sent candles for the
altar. The hunger for God in the children's eyes caused me to turn
to Jesus for a solution. I saw a great challenge from the Divine
Master in these little sheep. I went to visit him more often in
the Blessed Eucharist, pleading for guidance, knowledge and cour-

age. He told me, "Act with them as you believe I would if I were in your place." I realized Jesus was trying to teach and guide these little ones through my voice and actions. Representing Christ among these unfortunate victims of poverty, neglect and indifference gave me a feeling that he trusted me and had chosen me to draw others along the path to God's kingdom.

I decided that if I was to give the example of Christ to others, I would have to know him better myself. I felt there was so much I didn't know about the Savior, whose kindness and love had given me this new life. I increased my reading of the gospels, *The Imitation of Christ* and other books to help me grow familiar with the teachings of the Son of God. I bought catechisms for the children with donations I begged from friends. We prepared each child of Communion age for confession, taking the long hike to church after I had taught each one how to present himself to God for forgiveness. These children ranged in age from seven to 14. The poor little wooden parish church dedicated to St. Therese of Lisieux rocked with noise as I led these little friends of Christ into his Eucharistic Presence. Before the priest arrived, I gave them final instructions and led them in expressions of love for Christ as we prayed in a body.

The young curate arrived to hear confessions. I went last of all — listening to the rafters ring with noise. When I finished my penance, I saw the curate waiting for me at the church door. He said, "I couldn't let you go home without thanking you for this truly religious work. Don't let anything or anyone stop you. You have a way with children." I thanked him and asked him to pray for me. The pastor also came to me and said, "Keep up the good work. You are doing things for them I could never do. When I visit them, they discuss everything but God and their souls; they shy away from priests. If there is anything I can do to help, let me know." I told him I needed clothes, shoes and underwear for my little kids. Some refused to come to Mass because of their ragged clothing. I had told them that if I couldn't get clothes for them, I would wear clothes similar to their own, as long as they came.

Word spread that I needed help. Soon, secondhand clothing, shoes and books began arriving. Many Protestant people sent like offerings. Irma and I spent hours washing and ironing the clothes for our friends and their parents. Some of the families were quite large and had very little income. I went to the St. Vincent de Paul Society and received money to buy shoes and stockings for the children. The story of our work spread as far as Nova Scotia, and we got all the help we needed.

When I first brought these poorly clad children to church and tried to seat them for Mass, many people turned up their noses at them and hurt the children's feelings. I wondered what Christ thought as he witnessed these scenes. We were the object of much idle gossip and misunderstanding. Our curate heard about it and gave a long sermon on the meaning of Catholic Action. One Sunday he met me outside the church and led our little group to the front part of the church which had been marked "Reserved" for the little friends of Christ. Every Sunday I took care of the children alone, as Alderic couldn't come to help. I brought at least 50 on the long walk to public worship of their Creator. During some of the trials I endured in trying to bring Christ to these little ones, our Blessed Lord would often come to encourage and thank me.

On May 5, Alderic and I went by train to New Brunswick to witness the ordination of the young seminarian I had met in LeBlanc Office. This was the first ordination I had attended. As Lennie knelt before the bishop, I thanked God for the privilege of having played a small role in saving his sacred vocation. After Mass, I went to the altar rail, and this new priest came over to me and smiled. Joy filled me as he imparted his priestly blessing to me, after his parents and godparents. I visited with him in the afternoon, and he told me he was very glad that I had not become a lay brother; he felt that as a layman, especially a married layman with a family, I could do much for the cause of Christ by mingling with my brothers and sisters in the world. I invited him to visit us on his way to Moncton. A few weeks later he came to dine with us, and he consecrated our family to the Holy Family of Nazareth.

I continued to work with my little friends and was amazed at the ability Christ gave me to explain his doctrines. I soon saw our Lord extending graces to these children far beyond my expectations. At home they repeated what I told them, and it wasn't long before 90 percent of the parents began coming to Mass with their own children. It was no longer necessary to lead them all to Mass on Sundays. This reminded me of the biblical phrase: "And a little child shall lead them."

In June, I went to the Cathedral to make my profession, or lifelong promise to keep the rule of the Third Order of St. Francis. As I approached my assigned place from which I would be called to receive my black crucifix of profession, I was surprised to see a large delegation of children from my mission. They were scrubbed clean and dressed neatly by their parents who had arranged for them to represent the entire group. The Franciscan priest who accepted my profession told me later that he had heard of my work with these children, and he urged me to continue. He said in essence, "You are doing the type of work that the Franciscan Order has in mind in preparing its members spiritually to work for the cause of Christ." He quoted "one of the popes" as saying that the Third Order was a good school of Catholic Action.

When I wasn't working with the children, I made quiet efforts to reach anyone who would listen as I talked about the wonderful love God has for his children. I was delighted when, during one of his visits, our Lord made me understand how happy he was that my love embraced not only Catholics, but all the children of God. He made me aware that he was very pleased with many non-Catholics who were quite close to him and in whom he lived because of their wonderful sincerity and goodness of life. I used to wonder why he didn't draw them into the Catholic Church. But Jesus told me he had reasons of his own for allowing things to be as they were, and that people of any religious denomination would be judged on their good will toward him and on how they used the graces he had given them. I realized how truly vast is the family of God.

At the end of June, I was ordered to bed when rheumatic fever threatened me again; I had to spend six weeks in complete rest. I missed the children, but our curate said they were persevering in their new way of life and I should not be concerned about them. During my illness Jesus said to me, "I was hungry and you gave me to eat, I was naked and you covered me, I was thirsty and you gave me to drink." I was made to understand that he was talking about the thirst of souls for him, and he added, "Amen, amen I say to you, as long as you did it to one of these, you did it to me."

The War ended on August 15, and my labor exit permit was granted. We sold our furniture, for we were going to move in with Edith and Tony in Waltham. A Franciscan priest heard of my plans and asked me to reconsider, saying, "We could use you here to work for Christ." I explained why we wished to go, and he answered, "Then God's will be done, Roy. Perhaps he has other plans for you in the States."

The people of the village gave us a surprise farewell party, and one of the children gave me a pickle jar full of change as a farewell gift, to thank us for our efforts. It made them happy to hear that Irma would get a permanent with her share of the money, while I was to get a new hat. Before leaving, I received a special interior vision of St. Therese of Lisieux, who gave me to understand that she had been sent with the graces I would need to be a lay missionary for Christ. She also helped me to understand her autobiography, which, up to that time, held very little interest for me. Now I was able to penetrate the radiant beauty and splendid power of her heroic life, so completely consecrated to God.

On November 28, Irma and I, Sharon, and Irma's mother (who had come to help us) boarded a train for Massachusetts. I was a bit downcast as we left; a very beautiful, consoling chapter of my life had come to a close.

18. Steep Ascent and Rarefied Air

It was nearing midnight when we approached the American border. The immigration officer approved my permanent visa, and I whispered a silent prayer of thanks to God for this great favor. I had asked God for the privilege to live and die in America long before I had met my wife.

Irma was expecting our second baby in early February, and the trip was tiring for her. Shortly after we crossed the border, Sharon settled down, and we had a chance for some rest. We arrived in Boston and rode by taxi to the family house on Benefit Street in Waltham. Edith and Tony received us warmly and helped us get settled with our few belongings.

It wasn't long before we all found out that the worst thing that can happen to a married couple is to try to raise a family while living with someone else. Our situation easily became one of tension and misunderstandings. These circumstances were meant to teach me self-restraint, patience and charity, but I wasn't always successful.

Naturally enough, I was homesick for my native land, my family and friends. Added to this, I felt a growing homesickness for eternity. I tried to resist, with all my strength, the attraction for silence and solitude which had been plaguing me for some time. Jesus seemed to be constantly on my heels, calling me to a higher way of life, to a degree of spirituality that was obscure to me. Many times I begged him to leave me alone. I was confused, not knowing what he wanted from me.

I found work at a shoe-repair shop and did my share at home;

but in spite of my efforts, I found it hard living in America with people of different outlook toward God and life in general. As I bent over the machines hard at work in the shop, I endured a loneliness made bearable only by the fact that Jesus or the Holy Spirit would make his presence known to comfort and encourage me. Jesus told me that silence and solitude were necessary to my spiritual development, but the periods of silence and retirement I allowed myself didn't please my wife and others. I could see this quiet prayer was beneficial for my soul and indirectly good for them — it gave me a chance to stop and think about Christ and to try to look at things in my life from his point of view. Yet, Irma did not understand my self-imposed isolation. I wanted to be with her, but I was also convinced that I had certain spiritual needs which must be fulfilled. I had not yet learned how to reconcile these two drives, but Irma was patient.

On February 3, 1946, at 2:30 a.m., I was standing downstairs in the hallway of our home when I heard the cry of a newborn baby. Irma had presented me with our first son. We named him Roy Francis, for my Franciscan Father from whom I had derived so much help.

The day Roy was christened, Sharon was rushed to Children's Hospital with whooping cough and pneumonia. On that day Christ spoke to me and asked if I would accept it if he took Sharon from us. I said, "Yes"; but as it turned out, he was only testing me. She picked up good health rapidly. But then in September she started to limp. One morning I heard her crying. I went to her crib and saw her trying to reach up to the top of her bed and stand up. She couldn't raise her arms. I stood her up, and immediately she fell down. The whole side of her face was twisted, and her right arm and leg seemed paralyzed. Polio! We called the doctor but were unable to find anyone who would take her to the hospital! Everyone was afraid of contracting the disease. The doctor suggested that we take her to the Children's Hospital by taxi rather than call an ambulance. Irma wrapped Sharon in some blankets and took her to Boston.

Dark weeks followed. The doctors couldn't promise anything. Someone at the cobbler shop said, "Roy, you're always at Mass and Communion, and you seem to pray a lot; you never swear, you make visits to the Blessed Sacrament — and look what happens to you! If I lived like you and all these things happened to me, I would never pray again!" I answered, "God loves us, and he knows what he is doing. He is much wiser than we. Look at what he allowed to happen to his own Son and his Mother."

Jesus made his presence felt near me one day and asked if I would accept his will if Sharon came home crippled for life. I nodded my head in assent; I couldn't bring myself to say the word, "Yes."

Then, Irma found she was pregnant again. She was distraught: "How can I look after a little cripple and two small babies, too?" When our relatives heard about our distress, their advice was worthy of Job's friends: "The drugstores are full of ways, Roy; how stupid can you get?" We knew nothing about the rhythm method, and we didn't want to offend God; so, we clung to each other and loved each other in him, placing our trust in him. Somehow, we adjusted to the new pressures and the fear of growing destitute. We kept reassuring each other God wouldn't let us down. I told myself, "God can do all things," and together we hoped against hope for brighter days. One very bright day dawned when Sharon came home, saved by the doctors from permanent paralysis. For many years the Red Cross nurses gave her therapy, and today she shows no sign of her illness.

With so many tensions, Irma and I had many misunderstandings. When I disagreed with her or hadn't helped her enough, she was quick to say, "I hope you feel good and holy!" We seemed to be growing apart, without apparent fault on either side.

During our first month in Waltham, I had joined a Third Order Fraternity in Boston. I was named as a counselor on the board which determined the activities of the fraternity. Our membership came from all around Greater Boston, and I was instrumental in introducing 17 persons into the Franciscan way of life.

One night an archbishop spoke to our fraternity, saying that the Church was looking for saints to come from the working class. He said, "This doesn't mean you have to have visions, you know! I get so many people telling me about visions I begin to believe I am having them myself!" That brought the house down. I said to myself, "I will never tell a priest about these events in my life. They apparently don't trust people like me."

One morning on the way home from Mass, Jesus made his presence felt, and I said, "Why don't you let me tell one of your priests about all these visits of yours?" He told me that he would not like to see them frighten me away. He thanked me for trusting him, in spite of all the crosses he was asking me to carry. Indeed, these crosses gradually reconciled Irma and me. My strong urge to become active for Christ was renewed; but living in a strange city, I didn't know where to begin.

Jesus made me understand that he was the one who had given me this desire, and he would put it to use in his own good time. He told me that the chief means of converting souls was a life of prayer and union with him. With Irma's consent, I spent many evenings in private homes, talking to people who had invited me to discuss Christ's place in their lives.

One evening, while Irma was getting supper ready, I slipped upstairs to spend a few minutes of prayer in our bedroom. Then, in a way that I don't know how to describe, Jesus showed me the great power and eternal majesty of God. I trembled before him and felt as though my soul were being torn from my body in a strange flight into endless expanses of space. When I became aware of my surroundings again, I was in profound peace, a serenity which the world could not give me or take away from me.

Later, Jesus made me understand that he was the eternal High Priest, and that by my Baptism and incorporation into him I share in his royal priesthood. He told me that a secret life of prayer and sacrifice in union with his own is one of the best ways of exercising the priesthood of the laity. He informed me of the graces I was winning from his Sacred Heart; these would someday be applied to my active apostolate when he would call me to it. When others humiliated me, he made me realize that it was necessary if I were to be like him — meek and humble of heart. He taught me that humility is really self-forgetfulness and that the more I practiced this virtue, the more perfect my union of love with him would become. Humility would also make clear to me that the work of my sanctification was primarily his, not mine. If I remained lowly and submissive before him, there would be no barrier to his working in me, and, through me, in others. He made me understand that "praying without ceasing" is primarily the work of the heart and mind, and did not necessarily involve "lip prayers." I was grateful for his guidance in lending me these spiritual supports, as the spirit of the world swept over me, enticing me to live only for this world.

Irma and I found out that our views on marriage were the topic of many discussions at parties and club meetings. We were told quite frankly that it was cruel to bring children into the world when we had such limited finances, and that this was a greater wrong than interfering with the marital act. I asked myself, "Can so many people be wrong? Perhaps it is I who am out of step." I felt this way because I saw these people at Mass and Communion and helping in various parish works. Perhaps I was the victim of "crooked" thinking. The "full speed ahead" attitude of so many concerning the pleasures of the world appealed very strongly to me. My sex drive was so robust that many times I was tempted to hide my wedding ring and seek new horizons. At times, a single act of pure love for God would quiet these storms. At other times Jesus himself came to calm the roarings of the world, the devil and my human nature.

My wife, unaware of the temptations and trials I was undergoing — I found myself incapable of discussing them with her — often raked me over the coals, depriving me of my last source of human comfort. She didn't understand — how could she? — the path which I was walking. Sometimes I struck out in self-defense with impatient and harsh words. Then, regretting my behavior, I asked Christ to leave me alone. I protested that, whatever it was he wanted from me, he had picked the wrong man.

In those dismal days, I was greatly comforted by this passage from St. Paul: "With Christ I hang upon the cross, yet I am alive; or rather, not I; it is Christ that lives in me. True, I am living, here and now, this mortal life; but my real life is the faith I have in the Son of God, who loved me, and gave himself for me." I was particularly impressed by the apostle's solemn warning: "For if you live according to the flesh, you will die; but if by the spirit you put to death the deeds of the flesh, you will live." The words which immediately follow this warning especially pleased me, since I had never known a father on this earth: "For whoever are led by the Spirit of God, they are the sons of God; now you have not received a spirit of bondage so as to be again in fear, but you have received a spirit of adoption as sons, by virtue of which we cry, 'Abba! Father!' The Spirit himself gives testimony to our spirit that we are sons of God."

I realized I had a long, long way to go before coming to know the fullness of my divine adoption as a son of God. I was convinced that Jesus wanted me to arrive at the perfection of spiritual union with him. This burning conviction stayed with me in spite of the fact that I knew many Catholic couples who believed that Christian perfection or holiness could not be achieved in the married state. Many of them said, "Roy, what are you trying to do? You are not a priest or lay brother. You are a married man! You have to live like a married man!" They seemed to think that the physical expression of marital love was somehow an obstacle to holiness.

One day a friend asked me, "What were you doing at Communion today?" I said, "Why?" "Didn't you sleep with your wife last night?" "Of course," I answered. "Did you go to confession before Mass?" I told him I hadn't. "Well, if you slept with your wife last night and made love to her, how could you have the nerve to go to Communion this morning?" I tried to explain the sacredness of the marital act and that it becomes sinful only if husband and wife violate the laws of nature and of God; that the act uniting husband and wife is not only not sinful or something to be looked down upon, but is blessed by God in the sacrament of Matrimony. When I told him we give glory and honor to God by enjoying the pleasures of the married state, he was quite shocked. He missed the point I was making. "I go to Mass on Sunday," he said, "and I give money to the Church, but no one is going to tell me what I can or can't do in my bedroom!"

This pathetic statement reflected the thinking of many people who evidently think that their marital love has no connection with their love of God. They didn't see their mutual love as part of their association with Christ. This reminded me of one of my aunts in Canada who when taking a bath would turn all holy pictures to the wall.

If it hadn't been for the superhuman strength Irma and I received from Christ, I don't believe we could have stood up under the difficulties which filled our first years of marriage. We had entered marriage with very high ideals — and with much ignorance — and it came as quite a shock to find that neither of us had married an angel. We had strong wills and quite diverse temperaments, and it wasn't until we learned to surrender them to Christ that even a semblance of tranquility emerged in our home life.

One night, Irma said to me, "Honey, I want to talk to you. I had a very strange dream about you last night. You and I were standing in a huge crowd when suddenly from out of heaven came the most beautiful ray of light. It rested on you, and I heard a voice say, 'This is one of my chosen ones.' Honey, I can't explain what this has done for me. I'm sorry I've given you a hard time." We were at last beginning to understand each other; and, with understanding, love was free to grow.

We were helped by Irma's sister, Edith, who was an angel of mercy during the many illnesses which befell us. Coming to our rescue wasn't always easy for Edith, because her husband Tony often felt neglected and this raised some problems. In time, however, Tony became one of our staunchest friends and supporters. By way of trial and error and in the midst of problems every family must face, our married love found stability.

19. The Reaching Out of Love

In early fall of 1946, when Irma first told me that we were expecting our third child in May, we were barely able to get by on the $35.00 a week I was earning at the shoe shop. I kept my eyes open for a better-paying job, and one that would suit my still poor health.

There were times when things at home and at work got so rough that I wondered if it was all worthwhile. However, at this time Jesus was leading me to a new state of the spiritual life that was as hidden as it was comforting and consoling. It was hidden because only he and I knew of the growing union between us. He taught me that the simplest act of pure love was more pleasing to him than great deeds done without the motivation of love. In the far end of the finishing section of the shoe-repair shop, I spent thousands of hours bent over the burnishing machines, talking silently and lovingly with God in my heart.

While I was thankful for the consolations his many manifestations had brought me and the truths he had opened to me, I was most pleased because he had moved my will to surrender itself to him within the framework of "raw religion." I use this term because I was led to serve Christ in a manner devoid of emotionalism or sentimentality. I no longer sought or expected pleasant emotions when I rendered some service to God. I was learning to serve him in faith instead of feelings. Christ taught me that to follow in his steps I must do away with all timidity and compromise; my will must be determined to please him in all things. I was to accept and act upon the "hard sayings" of the gospel as well as those more pleasing and comforting to human nature. I came to understand that one can never make progress toward the heights of the mountain of God unless he walks by the side of Christ and relies totally on him.

I learned that the gate to the wonderland of God is the human heart, and the key to unlock it is our will. One does not arrive at this gate in the center of the soul without much labor and trial. Before one can even reach it, the way must be cleared of all the rubble we have allowed to get in the way of our advance toward God; and only hard work, along with the strength of Christ, will enable us to remove these obstacles. I found I was able to accomplish this "housecleaning" of the soul through the practice of rigorous interior penance and self-discipline.

Jesus revealed to me the meaning of his parable of the woman lighting a lamp and going about the house, searching every nook and corner to find a precious coin which she had lost. I recognized that this coin symbolized the wonderful liberty of spirit which comes from conformity of our will with God's. Jesus made me aware that I could not begin to enjoy the freedom of the sons of God until I had worked together with him in driving everything out of me that was incompatible with the purity and holiness he wanted in my soul. I realized, too, that it is not enough to work to give the heart a cleansing once and for all. The work of spiritual purification must go on continually, and we must use every grace we receive from Christ to keep our hearts clean.

In other words, the gifts of the Holy Spirit which Jesus brings to us cannot function completely without a struggle against the deeply rooted tendencies to sin which abound in our nature. The battle against these downward tendencies is endless. It must go on until death, even in saints. That is why Jesus warned all to "watch and pray," lest in moments of carelessness we be overcome by these rebellious traits from within.

There were times I was tempted to be satisfied with what Christ had already given me, but the challenge he kept extending to me urged me on and on. By his coaxing, Christ placed within my heart intensified longings to be united to him completely. And it was within the sanctuary of my heart that I found my greatest peace. God was teaching me to concentrate all my efforts on living every hour of every day in quiet conversation with him. In the stillness of my soul, he opened my mind to the harmony and life-giving elements of the whole of Christian revelation.

One of my joys came from realizing that the Christian Faith is the full development of Jewish beliefs. Thus I have strong spiritual ties with my Jewish friends, bonds even greater than my human affection for them. I felt close to their prophets and ancient leaders. Their faithfulness united them to the same God and Father whom I love and serve. Jesus made me understand that I bear some resemblance to the prophets of old, in that I have fought furiously to take possession of the kingdom of God. I had always admired the great manliness of the prophets and felt a close association with them, both in their human failings and their burning aspirations.

During our conversations, Christ would urge me to listen closely to him speaking through the scriptures and through his Church, that I might be firmly guided and strengthened for the struggles ahead. Several times I was comforted by the vision of a large group of saints. I do not know who these saints were, but I was given to understand that they were encouraging me to persevere until my entrance to their heavenly country came about. All these favors from God gave me much courage; without them, I knew I could not have survived the battles I was soon to face.

My awareness of the priestly dignity of the Christian life enabled me to come to the aid of my brothers and sisters in Christ, that they might come to know the fullness of joy in the Spirit of God. I begged our Lord to go where I could not go — behind the Iron Curtain, the Bamboo Curtain; into slums, broken homes, homes where sorrow reigned; into hospitals and prisons. I begged him to shower his love and mercy on all people afflicted and suffering, especially those who are prisoners within themselves, slaves of their own passions, locked within their own egos.

All this made me an active missionary of Christ in the world, even while I remained at my workbench and lived as the father of a family. It was God's way of showing that one does not have to be a priest or religious to do the great work of Christ — that all of us are called to this work, wherever we are in the world and no matter what our life's task. I knew there were many members of the family of God who were acting as the feet of Christ, their hearts roaming the world to bring his message to others. I knew there were many whose hands were the hands of Christ, ministering to the sick, the suffering and the unfortunate. I hoped that I was acting as the heart of Christ, loving and pleading for the children of God. I liked the definition of love given by a prominent psychiatrist: "Love is the opening of our life to another." Jesus knew that I wanted to go out into the world and with my words witness to him and his cause. He told me that he was pleased with this desire but that it was first necessary to be a witness to him where he had put me — with my own family, my co-workers, those in my parish and in my neighborhood; to these first I must be the witness of Christ. Our Lord told me that he would one day let me be, as it were, his mouth, speaking in public about the truths of his kingdom.

At the same time, as a layman — and an uneducated one at that — I was afraid I was trying to run ahead of God's guiding graces by entering into a work he didn't intend me to do. I didn't want to be a thorn in the side of his Mystical Body by speaking out unwisely or without due authorization. But Jesus reminded me of the incident in the gospels where his disciples told him that there was a man, not of their group, who was casting out devils in his name, and of his response: "Do not forbid him; for he who is not against you is for you." Our Lord indicated that when the time came for me to speak I need not worry about what I would say or how I would say it; the Holy Spirit within me would give me the courage and enlightenment to speak out without fear or indecision.

I also learned that our Lord wanted me to be a joyous person. I had observed in reading the lives of the saints the great joy which overflowed from their hearts, and this was surely the beauty of God's grace. Since my conversion to Christ, my life had become a wonderfully joyous experience; at last I could see the funny side of life. I realized that sadness is no virtue, that I must learn to control it. Sadness and gloom, like all the other unregulated passions of our nature, can spoil the balance of a well-adjusted personality. I was learning how to relax and enjoy the good things God has given us.

One day my boss invited me to attend my first major league baseball game. I hadn't known the capacity of the park, and I was breathless at the sight of so many human beings — 30,000, I was told — gathered in one place. I shouted and waved my arms, sharing in the wild enthusiasm of the fans. Yet, in the midst of my enjoyment, Jesus made his presence known to me and used my presence at the ball game to teach me a lesson in the spiritual life.

He said to me, "Roy, I know that you have been greatly impressed with the enthusiasm you see here. I would like to see this kind of enthusiasm for my kingdom, and I want it to spread all across the face of the earth. If only my followers showed as much enthusiasm for their spiritual life as they show in the enjoyment of temporal things, there would be a great renewal in the world of the zeal and fervor of the apostles after they had received the Holy Spirit. I want you to help spread this kind of enthusiasm to many others." This left me momentarily confused — how could I arouse such fiery enthusiasm for the things of God? I was reminded of that strange dream some years before, in which Jesus had come to me with his Blessed Mother, showing me a great multitude of souls whom I was calling to come and walk with Christ.

After this spiritual experience, I enjoyed the ball game even more. I felt that Christ had sanctified my recreation by his unexpected visit, and I thanked him for the many joys he was giving me. Irma told me she was happy to see that I was now beginning to enjoy the American way of life.

20. On Fields of Battle

May was approaching, and I needed money to pay for the delivery of our third baby. Someone suggested that I apply for work at a nearby shoe factory. With my experience as a cobbler, I was hired on the spot at double the wages I was getting in the shoe-repair shop. Little did I realize that God was leading me into circumstances where I would have to "stand up and be counted."

On my first day at the shoe factory, the personnel director took me to the assembly department and turned me over to the manager. He assigned me to a heel-seat cutting machine. My work had to be very accurate, or the shoes would turn out lopsided. He put me through a "dry run," cutting out the heel-seat on several discarded shoes. Once I understood what was expected of me, he brought over a rack full of new shoes for me to work on. It was a high grade of shoe, and I was afraid most of my week's salary would be paying for damages! I was glad to hear the 12 o'clock lunch bell.

As I began to eat, I was startled to hear a man shouting in a corner of our department. He was standing on a box speaking to about 60 persons seated around him in a large circle. He waved a bible vigorously as he called out, "If it isn't in the bible, I won't believe it!" I watched him with curiosity. Thinking this was a private meeting of a religious sect, I remained in a corner by myself, eating my lunch and watching him. He was a big man, like the lumberjacks I had seen in the Canadian forests and lumberyards.

As I began to relax from the morning's pressures, I was brought to my feet by the preacher's words, "The Catholic Church is a sanctimonious old harlot and mother of many bastards!" He said she had cut herself off from Christ by her activities in the early centuries and that those baptized by her were spiritually illegitimate. I tried to size up the situation. I saw that he had shaken several in his audience; they began protesting, and some made feeble attempts to answer his charges. The preacher must have noticed my expression, for he waved to me and said, "Come on over. We won't ask you any questions." I hesitated, partly from timidity, partly because I couldn't see any possible good coming from an encounter with him. I found myself wishing a priest were there. I waved my hand in a gesture of disgust and sat down, half-ashamed for refusing the challenge. I felt I was no match for this man who seemed able to quote the bible from cover to cover. He began taunting me with sarcasm and ridicule, "That's a good boy; listen to the holy Roman prostitute and beware of heretics!" I felt I had let Christ down as I watched the men and women looking up at this factory hand playing the role of messenger from God. I remembered how Jesus had often pleaded with me to help him win the hearts and minds of men. Here was my first major challenge and I had backed away in fear.

I prayed to the Holy Spirit for courage, then got up and walked toward the factory giant. Offering my hand, I asked, "What is your name, my friend?" He looked somewhat puzzled as he gave me his name. I said, "A real French-Canadian Catholic name, like mine!" He flew into a rage, shouting, "Don't link me to that hypocritical old whore!" With a calmness which surprised me, I asked, "Aren't you a Catholic?" He answered, "I was in her bloodstained clutches, but no more." "What happened, my friend?" "You call me your 'friend' after what I called your holy Roman Mother? I'll bet you would like to see me in hell!" The crowd looked at me, expecting me to agree. I answered, "I want to help as many as I can to avoid that awful separation from God. That's precisely why I came over here at your invitation, and also because I love you in Christ." This brought spontaneous applause from the crowd; one man put his arms around me, saying to the preacher, "God sent this kid here!"

An old Italian clasped his hands and danced around, shouting, "Angel! Angel!" then hugged me. I said to the preacher, "You claim you love Christ and serve him, yet you are insulting the very

Church he founded to spread his kingdom." He retorted, "Are you trying to say that people of other religions are going to hell?" "Indeed not," I said; "people of all religions who strive to serve God to the best of their ability according to the light of grace given them will go to heaven. I sincerely believe they are my brothers and sisters under God." "Don't you believe that all those outside the Catholic Church are lost?" I answered, "Anyone who tries to serve God by responding to all the graces given him by our heavenly Father, the Church considers to be his child. She prays for him and urges him to follow his conscience. She would have him enter into full communion with her and come to the knowledge and benefits of the full deposit of faith entrusted to her by her holy Founder."

He said, "Are you trying to tell me she is the only church Christ founded?" I said, "You are right. She is the only one that can trace her foundation to Christ. History shows that mere men founded all the other denominations and Christian sects. Just why Christ allowed divisions within his Church, I don't know; but I feel that no person of good will or sincerity will be excluded from his love, his mercy and his reward." He said, "Someone in your Church has stated that outside her there is no salvation. What do you say to that?" I answered, "I believe that he means that anyone who knowingly and deliberately resists the inspiration and light of the Holy Spirit concerning God's revelation to man will have to answer to God." He asked me, "Do you believe you are better in the eyes of God than a Protestant is?" I answered, "I believe there will be Protestants in heaven as well as Catholics, because I have known many Protestant people who, with their own deposit of the faith left by Christ, live better lives than some Catholics, including me." The factory horn blew, ending my first scuffle with the preacher.

When the next noon hour rolled around, the preacher called out, "Come, 'Angel,' and find the light!" I asked my friend where he had found Christ, the Light of the World. He pointed to the bible and said, "In the word of God." I said, "Who told you the bible is the word of God?" His face got red as he stammered, "Everyone knows this is the word of God." "I understand that," I said, "but who told *you* it was the word of God?" Absolute silence. There was a roar of applause from the once-frightened Catholics, who seemed to be gaining confidence. I said, "My friend, if you know your history, you remember that the early Catholic Church gathered the sacred writings and with the help of the Holy Spirit decreed them to be the word of God. The Church whom you attack

gave this bible to the world! Not everything Christ said and did is
contained in this book. St. John tells us that the world could not
contain the books if all were written down. When Christ ascended
into heaven, he told his apostles, 'Go and preach the gospel to every
creature, teaching them whatsoever I have commanded you.' You
are taking the word of the Catholic Church that this is God's word."
He answered me saying, "She used to be the Church of Christ, but
she isn't anymore. She fell into error and became corrupt." I cried
out, "You quote this holy book from cover to cover but seem to
have passed over many treasures on the way. Remember our Lord's
words to St. Peter, 'Thou art Peter, and upon this rock I will build
my Church and the gates of hell will not prevail against it.' Do you
call Christ a liar by telling us that error and the devil have prevailed
against his Church? You say you believe in Christ, but you must
believe his doctrines in the fullness of his revelation, or you cannot
truly say you are his disciple." I showed him reference after reference in the bible to the Church of Christ, and its four marks — one,
holy, universal and apostolic. He said, "I don't know what I'm
going to do with you! You must have been brought up wrapped
around the skirts of nuns!" When I explained my meager education
and background, this made him more angry.

The encounter with the preacher went on day after day. One
evening after work, a woman in her 40's followed me to the factory
gate. She said, "Roy, I'm a Catholic married outside the Church.
I don't blame the Church but myself for the state I'm in. I've been
praying for a year that God would send someone to shut this fellow
up. I've seen what he has been doing to the faith of these people,
and it made me sick. I knew a priest couldn't come to our rescue in
the factory and, thanks be to God, he sent you. I'm glad for the
sake of the younger ones; for myself, it's too late." I thanked her for
her confidence and asked her to keep praying. I told her that while
there was life there was hope and that she must place her trust in
God. There were several other Catholics who told me they were
very confused; some were about ready to leave the Church, since
they no longer knew what or whom to believe. I told them, "Can't
you see that the Catholic Church is the Church of Christ, not the
mother of spiritually illegitimate souls? Remember the long list of
holy men and women she has directed, nurtured and raised to the
heights of sanctity." I gave many examples, using the litany of the
saints and naming many prominent people in our own times who
lived dedicated, heroic lives for the cause of Christ and the good
of souls.

The preacher used every tactic imaginable to attack one doctrine after another. I told him one day, "The very cunning with which you try to trick these souls who are weak in faith and the sensuousness in which you couch your preaching, smell of the master of hell! I realize you have the right to follow your conscience, but I've been trying to find Christ in you, in your zeal, and I see little resemblance to him in your words and actions." I told one of the curates of our parish what I was engaged in, hoping he would tell me to stop. He said, "It is very important that every follower of Christ become articulate and, when the opportunity presents itself, do the best he can to defend the cause of Christ and his Church." He often asked me what techniques I used and how I explained the doctrines; he seemed satisfied and urged me to continue.

Over the months, my opponent's fervor gradually diminished. The spectators, now a hundred or more, began to ridicule him. I told them, "If you men and women are sincere in your search for Christ, this attitude is completely out of place; for we must love one another as he has loved us. We are not here to judge or condemn, but to state things exactly as they are." I admonished those of my faith for the apathy and indifference which had led them to almost give up their faith at the hands of this misguided man. One day the preacher began telling of immorality on the part of popes, cardinals, bishops, priests, nuns and Catholic faithful. He was surprised when I answered that I had read of some of this and knew of many other instances, one of which had even tempted me to leave the Church. I told him there was a difference between the divine character of the Church and the human nature of those called to be its members. The Church consists of both sinners and saints; Christ had stated that when the time came to judge he would sort out the good from the bad. "If some outstanding leader left the Church tomorrow, I would be foolish to leave the life-giving faith which Christ established. No one who really loves Christ likes to see him offended or his Church brought to ridicule by the actions of some of her members. But we must have the intellectual honesty to realize that we do not honor Christ by leaving a Church which has sinners in it. We honor him by staying in his Church, because we believe it is his Mystical Body and through it we receive his teaching, guidance and sanctification."

Word about our noontime discussions spread through the whole factory. Men and women came from other departments to join the group. I didn't like to see this happen, for I wondered what the factory officials would say. I was relieved when a friend of mine told me that two of the officials had said that what we did with our free time was our own business.

In the midst of all these activities, our third child, Susan Marie, was born. She was our healthiest baby, but Irma suffered massive hemorrhaging which brought her close to death. Thankfully, God chose to spare her, and she quickly recovered. When Susan was three months old, Irma became pregnant again. We calmed down after a while, shored up by the thought that, somewhere in the background, God was watching and would provide.

Many times I felt like giving up my apostolate in the factory, but Irma urged me to continue. As the battle raged, I was amazed at how God helped me to present the various doctrines of our faith to the factory hands, many of whom were immigrants who knew little English. Many of them told me that until I began speaking, Jesus had seemed just a remote historical figure. They were now learning that he was a living person and wanted to know him better and follow in his steps.

I gathered seven of the younger men who, I felt, were the most influential and instructed them at night in my home. I taught them the gospel and tried to instill in these young men love for the Real Presence of Christ in the Eucharist. I backed up my instructions with quotations from Sacred Scripture, working with them until the wee hours of the morning. My parlor was often filled with men seeking peace of mind. One night I got a call from one of the boys; he was playing pool downtown and had been talking about religion. Eighteen of his companions wanted to come over to learn how to know, love and serve Jesus Christ. Lest we wake my children, we met in an open field outside the city and talked until 2:30 that morning. The questions those boys asked! "Is Jesus really in church? . . . Does God really care about me? . . . What do I have to do to be good? . . . Is it a sin to hate? . . . Why is sex dirty? . . . What must I do to please Christ? . . . How can I control my passions?" Some said they went to church only to keep their mothers "off their backs." Apparently, finding God was a luxury they did not yet enjoy. Others said, "Roy, I wish you were a priest; you understand me so well . . . you give me hope and confidence in God . . . you make Christ real to me . . . I wish I could tell you my sins."

I taught them how to go to confession, sharing their happiness as they came out of the confessional smiling. Evening after evening, I taught them to follow Christ in every aspect of their daily living. If they fell back into sin and came to me discouraged, I sent them back to Christ's sacrament of Penance, reminding them of God's great love for them.

I saw the need for Catholic laymen to help Christ carry on his mission where his priests could not go. God's grace seemed to increase in these young men, for in their various walks of life they shared with others the knowledge and joy given them by Christ. Our pastor urged them to be apostolic-minded for the sake of Christ, and they responded.

One night, after instructing a group of teenagers, I made my way home alone. As I came to a bridge leading to our street, I became aware of the presence of a devil at my side. He said to me, "I've warned you many times to stop your work among souls that I want for myself. I'll get rid of you once and for all!" I felt myself lifted by a powerful force, trying to throw me over the side of the bridge into the Charles River. He taunted me, "I know you can't swim, and you will drown!" I said to myself, "Roy, watch your imagination!" until I looked down and saw a space of about a foot between my shoes and the sidewalk. I mustered all the physical and spiritual strength at my command and let out a heartrending cry, "Jesus!" At this one word, the enemy of Christ left me. Then Jesus came and restored peace, encouraging me to persevere in his cause and thanking me for what I was doing for souls. I told no one what had happened.

A few days later, I found my workroom cluttered with pictures of nude women. Another day, I found a pile of printed matter in which the celibacy of the pope, cardinals, bishops and priests was attacked and the Vatican Palace described as a gigantic house of ill-repute. Some of this material was in poetic form, filled with derision which seemed to be the work of a twisted and degenerate mind. I begged my newly formed lay apostles for prayers and plunged more vigorously into the battle. I examined every possible facet of Christ's teachings under the guidance of my parish priest and passed on to others what I had learned.

One day the factory preacher loudly announced that he was going to receive Holy Communion: "I'll bring that silly wafer of yours here and pound it with a hammer to show you that no blood or anything else comes out of it." Some who heard him made a variety of threats toward this poor man. After the crowd quieted down, I spoke to the preacher: "My friend, as you can see by the reaction of this crowd, you have pierced our hearts and minds by this attack upon Christ, the food of our souls. We are unworthy of his love and of his Real Presence among us, but we love this 'Wafer-God,' as you call him. We have it on his word that he chose this manner of remaining with us. You know that he proved his power over bread and wine and that he also called himself 'the Bread which has come down from heaven.' You believe in Christ, that he is God who let himself be hidden in the womb of a young Jewish maid. His executioners hammered away at his veil of human flesh and they couldn't grasp or destroy the divinity hidden in it. You know the story of Good Friday." When I finished, the crowd made the rafters ring.

I was overwhelmed with a deep sense of gratitude to the Holy Spirit, who had used a mere creature to defend the Eucharist and sustain the faith of these workers. Jesus then reminded me how he had sent me the Holy Spirit long ago in Canada. The preacher did not carry out his threat to desecrate the Sacred Host. I continued to expound my simple, workingman's theology until, by the grace of God, no one listened to my opponent anymore. A few weeks later, he abandoned his soapbox pulpit.

I seemed to be in the world, but not of it. One night I had a mysterious dream in which I walked the streets of Thompsonville, Connecticut. I saw the Blessed Trinity hovering over the town, filling a vast area between heaven and earth, and they were surrounded by a glorious multitude of angels. I saw St. John the Apostle leaning on the breast of Christ. They were seated at a table, in front of them the bread and wine of the Last Supper. The area over which this majestic vision appeared was to become the corner of Christ's vineyard in which I would labor.

21. The Price of Victory

In the early part of 1948, rumors spread in the shoe factory that the company was planning to move to Pennsylvania. We were expecting our fourth baby toward the end of May. I telephoned my brother, Fidele, who was still living in Enfield, asking if he could get me a job at the Bigelow-Sanford Carpet Mill. Following his instructions, I boarded a train to go there for an interview. I was hired immediately and started a new job as a weaver-apprentice. I arranged to live with Fidele and Mary until after Irma had her baby, as she wanted her own doctor to deliver the child.

Christ used this separation to teach me to lean on him alone. He taught me in many ways to bend always before the will of God whose ways I did not understand. He tested my will one day in a very painful manner. Toward the end of April, I received a phone call from Waltham, telling me that my wife had been rushed to the hospital a month ahead of time. I immediately made arrangements to go to Waltham. While changing buses at Worcester, I decided to call home and see how things were. Tony answered the phone and got all excited when he heard my voice. I asked how everything was and, instead of saying, "Irma's fine," in his excitement he said, "The *baby's* fine, but you will have to call the undertaker when you get home." "What happened to my wife?" I asked frantically. He only answered, "We'll tell you all about it when you get here," and hung up. I wanted to call back, but our bus was ready to pull out.

I was convinced that Irma was dead and our little ones were waiting for me without a mother. When I got to our street, I ran toward the house and rushed in shouting, "What happened? What happened?" My sister-in-law looked at me, white with fright. "Is Irma dead?" I cried. Edith shrieked, "What?" I told her about my conversation with Tony on the phone. She explained that Irma was fine but that the baby had died 20 minutes after being born. My legs wobbled and I sank onto the nearby couch. When I had composed myself, I went to the hospital to see Irma. She told me that the baby had been baptized and that she herself was at peace.

We buried our little Linda Rose at the foot of her grandfather's cemetery plot, knowing that she had gone to heaven from her new birth in Christ. We often pray to our little girl to plead for us before the throne of God.

Edith told me not to worry about the children; she would care for them and for Irma until they were ready to join me in Thompsonville. I returned to my job. During this period, I noticed that I had lost the sense of the presence of Jesus near me. I no longer had him to lean on. I found some comfort in his sacramental presence, but soon even that didn't seem to help. This left me with a twofold loneliness: far from God, and everyone who loved me. This new form of spiritual darkness started much the same as we see dark clouds announcing the arrival of severe thunderstorms.

I seemed to be penetrating further into the spiritual land to which Jesus had led me; but it was different now, for walking this narrow path I was without the sensible consolation of the presence of Christ. Once in a while in this strange spiritual wandering, Jesus would fleetingly show his face to me; and as I rushed toward him, he ran and hid. I often asked, "Why doesn't he leave me alone if he won't let me find him?" or "What have I done to you, Jesus?" I thought that Christ had lost interest in me.

These interior trials were more bearable after I read the *Spiritual Exercises of St. Ignatius Loyola.* This book showed me new practices of self-denial and gave me an increasing desire to walk courageously in the steps of Christ as he carried his cross before me.

In spite of my isolation from Christ, I was still able to counsel others. People still sought my advice, and God blessed my efforts. He fed them, yet seemed to leave me starving for divine love. I prayed to St. Therese and St. Francis of Assisi to help me find a priest in whom I could confide.

In September, 1948, Irma, the children and I moved into an old, rundown house in Somersville, seven miles from Thompsonville. In the summer of the following year, my wife and I got jobs on different shifts at the Somersville Manufacturing Company. I didn't like to see my wife having to work.

One day as I looked out the window of the mill, I was surprised to see the shoe factory preacher. I called to him; he looked up and exclaimed, "Well, I'll be damned!" I smiled and shook my finger at him saying, "Oh, oh, watch it, boy, you don't really want to go there!" He laughed. I asked him, "How's your new religion?" He put both arms in the air, waving them in a gesture of one who is fed up, and said to me, "No more, Roy, no more." "You gave it up?" "Yes, Roy, I'm all done." "Did you come back to the Church?" He nodded his head, waved a cordial good-bye and took off in his car. I whispered a prayer of thanks to God for helping this man who had been the object of my apostolate.

22. The Darkness of the Storm

In my search for Christ, I was often the object of severe attacks by the devil. He taunted me, "Here you are in love with Christ and you want to serve him, but for all you know, you may be one of those to be kept out of heaven. It looks that way, for you can't even find him anymore. You say you love him to the point of wanting to die so that you can be with him. You're very foolish, you know! You ought to enjoy this life, because you may be numbered among those who are to spend eternity in my company." Then he would present vile temptations, especially against purity, reminding me of my state before Christ came to lift me up. His filthy suggestions and discouraging insinuations about my eternal welfare shook me and made my loneliness for Jesus all the more acute.

The doctor urged me to see that Irma did not become pregnant, since it would be dangerous for her to have another child at this time. We knew nothing of the rhythm system, so we limited the marital act to two days a month. Being denied the comfort of our human love added greatly to my desolation of spirit. The sensual attractions of the world almost swept me off my feet. Irma and I suffered a kind of "dry martyrdom" in our efforts to be loyal to what we felt were the ideals of Christ concerning the holy state of matrimony. Many temptations came: "Come on, give yourself some pleasure in life! Without sex you will go crazy! Release your inhibitions! You may as well enjoy life! Maybe that is all the joy you will get to know! You are out of step with so many reasonable people!" I reminded myself that the bible says we are all called to be saints and that "sufficient for the day is the evil thereof." I would listen to Christ speaking through his Church and leave the rest to him.

To pull myself together, I made a retreat in the fall of 1949 at a retreat house run by the Passionist Fathers. I prayed, studied and rested but gained no relief from my troubles. For another year, I was plagued and tormented with the painful loss of the presence of Jesus. By late summer of 1950, my longing for Christ was reaching terrifying proportions. I was convinced that if someone didn't help me find him again, my grief over his absence would ruin my health. But no one understood what was happening to me. This, of course, was largely my own doing; I could find neither the courage nor the words to reveal my inner conflicts. The following psalm (143) portrays accurately my plight and the theme of my prayers for help through these years:

Yahweh, hear my prayer,
listen to my pleading,
answer me faithfully, righteously;
do not put your servant on trial,
no one is virtuous by your standards.

An enemy who hounds me
to crush me into the dust,
forces me to dwell in darkness
like the dead of long ago;
my spirit fails me
and my heart is full of fear.

I recall the days of old,
I reflect on all that you did,
I ponder your deeds;
I stretch out my hands,
like thirsty ground I yearn for you.

Quick, Yahweh, answer me
before my spirit fails;
if you hide your face much longer
I shall go down into the Pit like the rest.

Let dawn bring proof of your love,
for one who relies on you;
let it show the right road,
to one who lifts up his soul to you.

Yahweh, rescue me from my enemies,
I have fled to you for shelter;
teach me to obey you,
since you are my God;
may your good spirit guide me
on to level ground.

Yahweh, for the sake of your name
keep your promise to save me;
protect me from oppression,
love me, kill my enemies
destroy my oppressors,
for I am your servant.
—Jerusalem Bible

In desperation, I wrote to my priest-friend, Leonard, asking him to help me find my Savior again. He answered by telling me about his ministry in Northern New Brunswick. He thanked me for writing and begged me to continue doing so, saying my friendship was good for him and my letters made him want to be a better priest; but he made no reference to my plea for help. This convinced me I must be losing my mind and that this young priest thought so too.

I then wrote to Sister Marie Odile, who had shown so much kindness in years past, summarizing how Jesus had been dealing with me. She answered at once and encouraged me to seek a spiritual director: "My dear little Brother in Christ, take courage! Let us both pray that you will find a priest who will understand you." I saw the wisdom of her counsel; but how could I expect a priest to understand me, when I didn't understand myself?

One night, like a bolt from heaven, came a strong voice filled with divine authority. "Write! Write! Write!" As if in the grip of the Holy Spirit, I began writing feverishly. The thoughts came faster than I could put them down on paper as the eight years following my illness, the strange manner of my conversion, and my struggles to serve God spread out before my mind. I wrote three drafts before I was satisfied with the accuracy and coherence of the 27-page summary. I felt a great sense of relief; my painful secret was out at last, if only on paper.

I decided to write to the priest who had conducted my last retreat. I didn't know his name, so I addressed it to the Retreat Master; then I called to arrange for another retreat. I left for the monastery with a large manila envelope in my suitcase, containing my brief autobiography: my reckless and carefree days away from God; my fear of having lost my reason; the strange intervention of Christ in my life. In the letter I begged the priest to show me how to find the living Christ again, ending with these words, "I have heard of such things as religious hysteria, hallucination, auto-suggestion, etc., and I am very fearful of going on alone without the help of a friendly but cautious priest. I know Christ has promised to remain with his Church until the end of time. From these words of Christ, I know the Church won't lead me astray. I am ignorant of the higher forms of religious education, so I ask you to examine these pages and me. I don't want to use the gifts of God for my own destruction, nor do I want to lead others astray. I ask the Holy Spirit to guide you and beg him for the grace to follow your direction."

I arrived at the retreat house and unpacked; then I took my story and went to the chapel. Kneeling on the top altar step, I said, "Well, Lord, here I am. I have followed your advice." I held the envelope up in front of the tabernacle, asking him to bless it and give the retreat master and me all the graces we would both need to do his will. I genuflected and left for the front door of the monastery. As I rang the doorbell, I noticed over the door a carving of the instruments of the passion of Christ — an exact replica of what I had been shown in a strange dream. I looked through the glass and saw a little, white-haired priest coming toward me. I was startled to hear the same voice that had commanded me to write: "Give your story to this man!" I entered the lobby and stammered my name. "Can I help you?" the priest asked reassuringly. "I am embarrassed, Father." "Why so?" "I addressed this to the retreat master, and a voice commanded me to give it to you as you came to the door." He showed no sign of how my words affected him. I held out the envelope and said, "I hope you will be able to help me get my bearings." He opened it and smiled. "Isn't this strange, Roy, you wrote this on my birthday?" He asked a few questions about my life, then told me to come back Sunday morning at eleven. He took me through the monastery to the retreat house, where I spent three days of prayer, instruction and rest.

Sunday morning, the priest who had accepted my manuscript led me to a small but comfortable counseling room. He was Father Frederick, then 60 years old. Excusing himself for a moment, he came back with my manila envelope and a book, then sat opposite me. "First I must tell you, Roy, that you mustn't be afraid anymore. After careful consideration, I am convinced that these things you wrote about come from God. I think he is preparing you for some special kind of work. He has been very good to you. I would say he seems very pleased with you, and in turn you must continue to show him generous love. My advice to you is this: don't act any differently than you have been doing. Keep trusting him, no matter what happens. If you want me to, I will be happy to be your spiritual director." I said I would be very grateful if he would guide me. He said he thought two visits a month would be sufficient and he would hear my confession if I so chose. He then handed me a little red book, *The Mystical Life of Graces.* I knew what "graces" meant, but I wasn't sure of the word "mystical." Father Frederick said, "I could explain your path to God, but to save time I want you to read that book carefully. It was written by Heronius Jagan, a lay-man who had experiences similar to yours. He did a good job of writing it. We use it for our students." I went to confession, then thanked my new friend to whom God had directed me.

I stopped at the chapel to thank our Blessed Lord for this singular grace — I felt I had been talking to a saint. Then I took a walk in the monastery garden. Father Frederick had suggested I use that area to read the book, where no one could see what I was reading; he asked me to keep my secret from everyone. I walked along the peaceful paths and began to read. The extraordinary graces God had given to Jagan were the graces he had given to me. I felt a great sense of relief as I saw that my fears of mental imbalance, eight years in the building, were completely unfounded.

In the spring of 1951, Sharon made her First Holy Communion. Father Frederick, a gentle man of God, invited us to the monastery. My wife and family became attached to this wonderful priest, who instilled his burning zeal in the hearts of our little family.

The central theme of living and acting was what he called "affective" and "effective" love of God and neighbor. You might say that it amounts to putting affection into practice, showing our love by serving God and man in the spirit of the great commandment Jesus gave us. It is a spirit of loving service. "It's as simple as that," he used to say. He kept urging me on to a stronger practice of the theological virtues of faith, hope and charity and encouraged me to have childlike confidence in God, whose ways are not our ways and whose thoughts are above the minds of men. He told me one day, "Be patient, Roy; Jesus will return when he has accomplished in you what he desires. He knows you have this painful sense of absence of your divine Friend." Several other men who had come to me for direction and counsel I turned over to Father Frederick's skillful care.

Under his wise direction, I tried to acquire the virtues that would make Jesus feel more at home in my soul. He urged me to let my love of God overflow into an active apostolate, to help Christ win souls. He used many books to teach me the secrets of the spiritual life and how to apply God's graces to my vocation as a Christian father. Father Frederick steadied my spirit, which had been faltering on the dry, dark desert of God's "absent presence."

I began to experience a very painful piercing sensation in my hands and feet. Father Frederick advised me to soak them in hot water and Epsom salts. I followed his advice, but the pain got worse. Through an interior illumination, Jesus later told me that he had drawn me into a very intimate sharing of his Passion; the pain I had been feeling was from him. Jesus led me into the darkest area of the spiritual countryside — where I wandered four years with the mysterious pain in my hands and feet, a feeling I can only describe as though red-hot spikes had passed through them.

I gave over to Christ, through his Blessed Mother, all the merits of my life and all the riches I had received, so that I could go to God in complete poverty and nakedness of soul. I consecrated all my goods, material and spiritual, to him. During my lonely journey, the psalms came to mean much to me as a source of strength and courage. Many of them expressed exactly what I was experiencing in the depths of my soul.

I continued my activities in the lay apostolate, trying to help others express their love of God by helping their neighbor. Jesus gave me the grace to do this in many different ways. I led pilgrimages to various local shrines and drew many to the Franciscan way of life in the fraternity at St. Michael's Cathedral in Springfield. In all these activities, Jesus continued to allow me to share in his sacred Passion through the mysterious crucifixion I was undergoing. I then understood an event which had taken place before these great sufferings began.

One morning as I knelt in our dining room for my meditation, I tried to picture the scene in the garden just prior to the arrest, torture and death of Jesus. What I had expected to be a quiet meditation turned out to be a startling sharing in the living reality. Fully conscious, I found myself standing in the garden, watching Jesus. He was on his knees, leaning against a huge boulder. He seemed so sorrowful, so weak, so afraid. I saw him rise up and stagger over to the sleeping apostles and ask them to watch an hour with him. Twice he went to them, and finally I heard him say sadly, "The spirit is willing, but the flesh is weak."

I ran over to him as he was leaving the apostles and put my arm around his shoulders to comfort him in his fright and sadness. I tried to steady him as I led him back to his place of prayer. As he knelt down this time, he broke out in an awful sweat of blood which drenched his clothes and trickled to the ground. I murmured words of compassion for him and told him of my great love. I assured him that I would never leave him alone and that I wanted to help him. I used my handkerchief to wipe the bloody sweat from his face.

Then I stepped back as Jesus became absorbed in his prayer. I heard him say, "Not my will, but Thine be done!" I was surprised to see an angel appear, give him a chalice, then vanish. After he drank of the chalice, he arose and extended his chalice to me. I backed away, for I could not bring myself to drink from the cup of Christ. He came closer and offered it to me again. Not wanting to seem presumptuous, I refused again. I wanted to please Jesus, but I couldn't place my lips to that holy chalice. I was shocked into action when Mary, the Mother of Jesus, appeared and said, "Do as my Son tells you!" I reached to accept the chalice from the hands of Jesus. Offering it to me, he said, "If you want to follow me and help me, you must share in the chalice of my suffering." As I raised it to my lips, I saw that Christ had drunk half of his bitter cup. I drained every last drop, not knowing how I could help my Savior bear the burden of his terrible suffering. Then I found myself again kneeling in the middle of the room in my house.

When I told Father Frederick, he said, "Very good, Roy, very good. Jesus is preparing you for even greater suffering and closer union with himself." Jesus did not welcome death as something desirable; he accepted the will of his Father. He knew that the sacrifice of himself was the means of leading souls to his kingdom. If I were an adopted son of God, I must be made like his own Son in every way, even in his suffering.

23. The Strength of Reassurance

I knew that true happiness — another word for holiness — lies in fulfilling God's will perfectly. For me, that meant living the life of an average American father, doing all the things with my family that any father does. I tried to teach my children how to love God and to express that love in all the circumstances of everyday living. We shared the joys of any family: ball games, movies, birthday parties, hikes, swimming. The children learned the value and importance of work as they kept our grounds neat and did their chores around the house.

Like many American fathers, I participated in civic and social activities, and attended all sorts of meetings. When the children became scouts, I helped with their various projects — a challenge to any father. Irma enjoyed a full social life, occasionally going to plays and visiting neighbors and friends. I was able to enjoy a good laugh and be happy, enjoying the time I spent with my wife and children. I was living a full and rewarding life.

However, this did not alleviate the painful longing of my soul to see and be with God forever. I was still, in a real sense, alone, even when surrounded by my dear family. I was unsatisfied even when flooded with consolation. I attempted to fill the emptiness in my soul by more frequent conversation with God, rising at five in the morning to recite the Divine Office. While praying the psalms, all my petitions and desires for the whole world were included in the united prayer of the Church.

I knew that in taking care of the seemingly endless details of life I was doing God's will; yet, most of the time these duties were oppressive to my spirit. My mind and will were so centered upon God that all the joys of nature and even the happiness of family life couldn't satisfy my hunger for God.

The apparent absence of Christ made me wonder if there were some hidden sin or offense which made me feel rejected. This led to a period of scrupulosity; I became overly anxious about myself and the condition of my soul. This was brought on in part by the memory of my sinful past. I was haunted by a terrible fear that I was not in the state of grace, that God did not love me anymore. I often wondered if I had any faith left.

I spoke to a priest who had heard my confession, begging him to let me go over my past life with him. This he would not let me do. This fear of God's rejection went on for years, almost without any comfort or consolation. Meanwhile, I was severely tempted to despair.

One day, while sitting near one of the machines at work, I was nearly overcome by a sudden attack of evil thoughts. Tears flowed down my cheeks as fierce temptations raged at my soul. I felt that I was offending God whom I loved and wanted so much. This dark moment was brightened by a sudden and unexpected visit from Christ. He appeared as the Carpenter of Nazareth and stood at my right side. He said, "Roy, do as your priest tells you to do. In listening to him, you are listening to me, for I sent you to him that he might guide you in my name. I want you to forget the past, for I am not 'yes' and 'no' at the same time. I do not want you to be sad but to rejoice in your religion. I do not want you to allow any of those fears concerning the state of your soul to oppress you."

He made me understand that it was only because I loved him very much that I was so concerned about offending him. He told me he was with me at all times, although I was not aware of it, and that he was not only concerned about my spiritual welfare, but was personally protecting me from many accidents during my working hours. He told me that he observes all men in all their actions and that he has a very special compassion for fathers who take on strenuous labors to fulfill their role as heads of their families. I understood that Christ the Worker was well aware of the blood, sweat and tears that fill the lives of those who work for a living. Our Lord departed from me as suddenly as he had come, leaving me with an inner peace and security. I recalled the words of St. Paul:

"Rejoice in the Lord always; again I say, rejoice!"

As the months rolled on, I kept up all my activities to help spread the kingdom of God in the hearts of others. I realized, as I read Christ's life in the gospels, that he was not only a man of action but also a man of prayer. I took his advice to "come aside and rest awhile," and often sought refuge in a retreat house. I attuned my soul to the whisperings of the Holy Spirit, who Christ had promised would be our Comforter and the Father of the Poor. I listened to Christ's sacred doctrines preached by his priests. Freed from the pressures of work for a few days, I had a chance to study Jesus and asked God to help me acquire some of his virtues. I begged him to pour out upon society the graces it needed, that all its activities would be pleasing in his sight. I prayed for his clergy who carried a heavy burden and asked him to sanctify husbands, wives and families.

In the fall of 1951, I returned to the retreat house of the Passionist Fathers. I felt a keen sense of intimate love for Jesus Christ that made me tremble with fear of losing him. I had just heard a sermon on the human tendency toward sin, and I felt there might be something in my soul keeping me from God. Troubled, I went to the chapel and asked a priest to hear my confession. I told him of my intense love for Christ and how I lived in fear of ever offending him again. He saw that I was trying to be sincere to the point of scrupulosity. He said, "I am sure that God is satisfied with your efforts. To put you at peace, I tell you that I absolve you in the name of God from all your sins, just as they stand in his eyes. Go in peace." This statement made in the name of Christ brought me much comfort. I went to my room feeling that a great weight had been lifted from my shoulders.

The moment I entered my room, I became aware of the presence of what I felt to be Satan. I fell to my knees, telling Jesus I loved him. I was once more filled with the fear of losing God through mortal sin. I knew this was a possibility because of my frail human nature. The devil came to me with unspeakable hatred and said, "You may be enjoying the peace and love of Christ, but I know how weak you are, and I will keep at you until you finally give up and go back to your old habits. Go ahead, enjoy this retreat, but you will sin again." I was tempted to despair. As much as I loved life, I was willing to die right there, alone in the dark, rather than go on living with the likelihood of offending my God in the future.

Satan filled my imagination with various scenes, trying to convince me that I would one day become a great sinner. I remembered the days when I had walked the road of life without belonging to Christ and again began to fear that I would never rise above my human weakness to the love that Jesus wanted from me. I felt certain that the many favors he had mercifully given me would be wasted and ruined. How could I be of any value in his cause? I could not see it! The devil tried to convince me that I was already lost; in my imagination, he even showed me as I would be — suffering the pains of hell.

As I was tossed about in this confusion, I heard the voice of Jesus say, "I am here." Before I lifted up my head, I knew that Christ was standing at the foot of my bed. I got up on my elbow, and I was filled with great joy at seeing my beloved Jesus again. He told me once again of his love for me. The more he spoke of his love, the more miserable I became, and I told him that I was overwhelmed by the fear of offending him.

Christ listened with great compassion, then invited me to draw near to him. Feeling my unworthiness, I hesitated. When he saw this, he approached closer to me and said, "Roy, look into my heart." He had opened it wide for me. He said, "What do you see?" I answered, "I see patience, mercy, kindness . . ." and I wanted to tell him all the things I saw. He interrupted me and asked, "But what is the most striking thing you see there?" I broke into a happy smile of childlike delight at what I saw — the love within his heart, love overflowing for me and for all men. I answered, "I see love." Then he said, "Roy, you shall never fall from grace again!"

Our Lord spoke with majestic finality. I was filled with astonishment. In my own mind I began formulating the question, "Jesus, why are you giving me this tremendous grace?" But before I could put the question into words, he answered, "Because you love me so much." Before I could formulate my next question, "Jesus, who asked you to give me this great favor?" He gave me the answer with these words, "My Mother begged this grace for you." As he said this, he motioned to his right, and there I saw our Lady standing, radiant and serene. Jesus then held his arms out to me and drew me close to his Sacred Heart.

In that moment, I began to understand how much he loves all mankind. I put all my fears, doubts, coldness of heart, my trials, hopes, sorrows — everything — into the gentle heart of my Savior. Realizing that he was confirming me in grace and promising me heaven, I talked with him about my family, my mother, brothers and sisters, stepfather, and the many people I wanted to help bring to heaven. My Lord answered, "Roy, you take care of my interests, as you have been doing, and I will take care of yours!"

Our Blessed Lady was pleased at the great gift I was receiving from her divine Son. Many times during the painful years when I felt abandoned by God, Mary had come fleetingly to comfort and encourage me. I expressed my gratitude to Jesus and his holy Mother. Then they left me. Peace was once again restored to my heart, and I was filled with new spiritual and physical energy. I went home from that retreat renewed in the Spirit of God, ready to resume my duties and to face whatever lay ahead. From that moment to this, my worries have never truly bothered me.

24. Pains of Purification

There followed several months of spiritual refreshment and peace. Then I was again engulfed in dense spiritual darkness. I seemed to be walking in that very dark region he had shown me years before when he revealed the land through which I would have to make my spiritual journey. I later learned that this darkness of spirit was caused by my approach toward the hidden God who abides in the very center of my soul. I was in darkness because my soul was not yet purified enough to gaze upon Eternal Light.

I was finding out what God is NOT. He is not image, form, or anything that can be explained by words or pictures. I was beginning to see that he is pure spirit, dwelling in inaccessible light. My new knowledge of God filled me with a correspondingly deeper knowledge of self, and so I discovered the indescribable, immeasurable distance between my Creator and myself. I saw that I was a simple creature, filled with impurities and blindness which prevented me from gazing upon a God of purity and light. In this darkness of spirit, I became ever more painfully aware of my weaknesses and sinful inclinations. My slightest imperfections were shown to me, and I discovered how far I was from the perfection and purity of Jesus. I could not bear the thought of my past sins; I felt they were responsible for keeping my Lord away from me. I felt once more that he couldn't possibly want anything to do with me. In spite of the spiritual infirmities which were still mine, my loving God kept drawing me on toward him. I resisted; the realization of my hitherto unknown spiritual defects was holding me back. I began to learn from this experience what Christ meant when he said that nothing defiled can enter heaven.

For several years, with all my striving, I seemed to make little progress in climbing the heights of the mountain leading to God. I knew I would have to undergo much more purification, similar to that which the souls in purgatory must suffer before they can be admitted into the full, joyful vision of God our Father. Thus I saw purgatory as a place of great love, where God mercifully removes from souls all those things which would prevent their enjoyment of him in heaven.

During this period of suffering, I tended to look for and lean upon natural and spiritual consolations. Yet, even when these were granted to me, my spirit remained empty and dissatisfied. During this time, I was made aware of the Holy Spirit living within me, and I learned to lean upon him for strength, support and consolation. I knew the Holy Spirit was even more anxious than I to see my soul purified and made ready for the sight and enjoyment of the Most Blessed Trinity.

One evening in the fall of 1955, after watching television for a while, then reciting the Divine Office, I knelt in quiet adoration of the Holy Spirit within me. After several minutes of silent love between us, I blessed myself and, with a deep inner peace and joy, went to bed. I do not know how long I had been asleep, but I was aroused by the most terrifying experience of my life. I bolted upright in my bed when I heard, deep within me, bloodcurdling screams and awful cursing. These were not audible sounds, for I saw through the open door across the hall that my children were sleeping. I was aware that my soul was being attacked by a horde of evil spirits, uttering the most foul language, and using the name of Jesus in hatred and contempt. These evil spirits seemed to fill every sense of my being. What pained me most was that these demons were trying to make my tongue join them in ringing out the basphemous words with which they filled my mind.

I underwent the awful torment of a demoniac, or a man intoxicated with evil. If all the embittered people of the world were put in one place, and all together cursed God in their rage, the noise and horror of it all could not begin to compare with the noise and hatred that I experienced in my soul that night. I was convinced that I was witnessing the hideous torments of the damned, and I was afraid that they might succeed in forcing my tongue to join their chant of hatred and despair. Yet, of one thing I was absolutely sure: the devils had not succeeded in penetrating to the center of my soul where God dwells. My will was sheltered from their attacks. They could only fill my external senses with their cursing hatred of God in an attempt to have me join them. Instinctively, I sought refuge deep within the center of my soul, in God's holy presence within me. I realized that my will could be moved by no one but God or myself. I felt secure, even though I felt that I was being tortured by the inhabitants of hell.

The demons were filled with jealousy of what God had been doing for me over the years. They had somehow become aware that I was about to receive special blessings and graces from almighty God. Unable to move my will against the God who loved me so much, they flew into a violent rage against me. When they had exhausted themselves in pouring out the vileness of their hatred on me, they left in a screaming rage. For some time after, the hallways of my mind echoed with their frightful cries, moans and turmoil. Once again, I felt sure I must be going insane.

Then I sensed the presence of Jesus bending over me to comfort me. He said, "Be at peace, Roy. I allowed this to happen to you for a very good reason." In that instant, my entire being enjoyed a wonderful calm. I thanked my Savior and immediately fell asleep.

This event impressed upon my mind the necessity of much prayer and penance and the need to stay close to Jesus through the Mass and the sacraments. I was given a better understanding of the triumphant victory of Christ over the powers of hell by means of his Passion, death and resurrection. I was grateful to our dear Lord for establishing his Church to keep these monstrous beasts of hell in check. I also understood better the words of St. Peter, who warned: "Be sober and watch, for the devil goes about like a roaring lion seeking those whom he may devour."

I was filled with the strong desire to become a closer partner of Christ in this combat with an adversary who will never give up his struggles to capture our souls. At the same time, I became more aware than ever of the need to protect myself from this cunning and powerful spirit by developing stronger faith, hope and love for God. I was given to understand that if I did this, I would be safe from the attacks of hell.

As the years progressed, I was grateful to God for having shown me how to deal with Satan, for he tempted me violently against the values of faith, hope and charity. There is no earthly battle, no matter how bloody or horrible, that can compare with the violent fighting which takes place among the forces of the spiritual realm. This war began, as the bible tells us, when the angelic army of God fought the rebelling spirits. The battle will go on until the end of time, until each soul has been won to God or lost forever.

The memory of this dreadful scene showed me the unmeasurable mercy of God who had drawn me from the pathway leading to such torments. At the same time, I shuddered when I heard men joke about the devil and hell. It was no laughing matter.

I knew that God wanted me to love him in others, so I did everything in my power to worship and love him in his abiding presence in other human beings. If I met people for whom I could not render some personal service, I adored God in the living tabernacles of their souls. I became acutely aware of his presence in them, and this made his apparent absence from me all the more painful. I continued to rise early in the morning to render worship to God the Father through the prayers of the Divine Office.

Despite my prayers, I no longer gained consolation from the doctrines of my faith as I had in the past. Hope also seemed to abandon me. I seemed to have nothing to hope for, or to hope in. Most painful of all, I thought I did not love God anymore and that he had lost his love for me. I was stripped of everything; I felt spiritually naked. I was greatly concerned that God be loved, honored and glorified by all the people I met, though I felt sure that I could no longer do this in my own life.

At the same time, I hungered so much for God that death at any moment and under any circumstances would have been welcome. Still, I thought that if he should call me, I would have nothing to bring him; my soul was the poorest thing in God's creation. As I instinctively surged toward the One who was drawing me, I nonetheless felt like a lost soul. Yet, with my spirit crushed and groveling in the dust, I somehow kept my uncomprehending trust in God.

My mind underwent great torments, and Jesus made me aware that he had placed an invisible crown of thorns upon my head. For a year and a half I experienced a sensation of bleeding within my head. The blood seemed at times to go down into my throat and nauseated me. I told my wife about it and we went to two doctors who could find no reason for this strange sensation. Added to the interior sufferings of my soul, God allowed me to suffer from a severe stomach ulcer which compounded my misery.

I continued going to Holy Communion on Sundays and as often as I could during the week. Even Holy Communion gave me no comfort nor did it quench my thirst for Christ. I began to think that I must have displeased him greatly for him to leave me so alone.

There had been times when, in the absence of Jesus, our Blessed Lady would come very briefly, clasp me in her arms to soothe the pains in my head and encourage me to persevere. But now even she had joined Jesus in hiding from me. I hungered for God; and yet, though I was a captive of his love, I also felt I was a captive of his anger. God alone knows how I still managed to live a normal life at work and with my family.

I found it hard to pray. I used to sit in church and plead with Christ to talk to me, or at least give me some indication that he still loved me. I was answered with silence. I was ready to suffer any illness —anything that Jesus wanted from me. But there was one thing he was asking that I wasn't ready to give: the total abandonment to his divine will of everything I had, and was, and desired to be. There seemed to be one reservation still within me: that if I followed this strange path along which God was leading me, I would lose my sanity.

The devil used all his powers to fill me with anxious fear and even suggested that religion taken seriously would drive me into a fanatical craze. He continued to drag me through most painful temptations against purity, charity, patience and so many other virtues. One night, listening to two friends talk about the great joy and peace they had found in serving God and how close he was to them, I was depressed that these men who had been led to Christ through my efforts were enjoying him, while I seemed to be utterly rejected. My memory was blinded to all the wonderful things that God had done for me in the past.

One day Jesus spoke to me in a mysterious manner, "If by turning over the use of your intelligence to me, you would please me and help me save many, many souls, would you do it?" I was appalled at the mere thought of "losing my mind," even to him. He asked me the same question again. I loved him, and it pained me to think of refusing him, yet I said to myself, "This is a lot to ask." Again Christ said, "Will you consent to this type of suffering should I allow you to lose your mind?" At last, I cried, "My Jesus, I love you and I cannot refuse you anything. I trustingly throw myself on your mercy and love, and I abandon all into your care. My sanity is most precious to me, but if by taking it from me you will be glorified and souls will be saved from hell, then, Lord, it is yours."

He continued to let me walk in darkness of spirit, and I was convinced that everyone on earth was pleasing to God except me. No matter how sincerely and eagerly I tried to grow in virtue, I seemed to be backsliding. Whenever I heard the hymn, "Nearer My God to Thee," I became sad. I did not know how much more I could bear, but I made up my mind that I would persevere in doing the best I could, even if God made me live the rest of my life this way.

One day, in an interior manner, Jesus told me he wanted me to write the story of my life and make it known to the world. Write my life story? I couldn't see what good this would do. But I told Father Frederick of this request of Christ, and he said, "You have my consent. I think it is a very good idea." "But Father," I protested, "how can I, with a sixth-grade education, write a book?" He said, "You just tell it as it happened and leave the rest to God. It will not be easy for you, Roy, but God has many ways of doing things."

In my sleep one night, Jesus came to me, accompanied by three saints. In this comforting dream, I was kneeling in the rear of my parish church, looking at the tabernacle, making acts of love to Christ, and filled with a terrible fear of deserting him through sin. Suddenly, I saw the whole altar and sanctuary ablaze with the rays of a piercing light of many colors, which seemed to come from beyond the earth. Then I saw Jesus standing at the altar, facing me. On the gospel side, to his right, stood St. John the Evangelist, the apostle whom Jesus loved, clothed in yellow and brown. To the left of Jesus stood two saints, whose names I do not know. I got the impression they were priests, for they were dressed in cassocks. One of them stood next to Jesus, at the epistle end of the altar; the other one, on the second step, beckoned to me to enter the sanctuary.

As I approached, the priest on the lower step reached up and, putting his arms around my shoulders, led me to the feet of Christ, saying, "Lord, here is one who is fearful of offending you." I knelt at our Savior's feet. Jesus leaned over me and put his hands gently upon my shoulders, while I looked up into his face. I poured out my love for him, and he listened silently. He returned my gaze of love, and with his hands still resting on my shoulders, he said, "Roy, I've been watching you." Having spoken these words, he pierced my very soul with his gaze. I felt that he had searched out the deepest recesses of my soul. I had the impression of being judged. Whatever he saw in me, he seemed to be content. With a parting glance of love, he took his hands from me, straightened up and turned toward the tabernacle. His friends did likewise and all disappeared in the glorious light from which they had emerged. When I awoke, I was at peace for the first time in years.

Jesus made me aware that the three saints had been interceding with God on my behalf during my suffering. I was determined to follow Christ into that glorious light where he dwells with his friends. He continued to refresh my spirit with momentary visits. When he was near, nothing else mattered, no matter how painful. I often begged Jesus to make me a victim of his love, that I might help him win souls for our Father in heaven. I was learning more and more that the only way to God is that of the cross. I was now able to embrace willingly any cross placed on my shoulders by Christ.

My wife, too, had learned how to carry the cross with quiet courage. I learned much from watching her bear the burdens of a wife and mother through the years of our marriage. At times, I was sure that I added to the weight of her cross.

For several years, my wife and I denied ourselves the physical expression of our human love. This was necessary because of Irma's poor health and also because we felt we could not properly support another child in our poor circumstances. Whenever mutual passion threatened to overwhelm us, we calmly talked over the situation. We realized the great need of husband and wife for the marital embrace; yet, through prayerful determination to follow Christ we succeeded in practicing continence.

During a particularly hard period of family illness and financial problems, I asked Father Frederick if I might tell Irma of my life with Christ. I explained that since my wife and I were as one person before God, it would perhaps encourage her to know what God was doing for me. Father Frederick consented. When I told Irma of Christ's visits to me, she was delighted to hear of God's great love for our family and the many special graces he had given me. I then told her that I was to make Jesus' love for mankind known by writing about my experiences.

Writing my life story was not easy, and I owe a great deal to Irma's encouragement. She knew my sensitive nature, and saw that I was struggling against great obstacles. I was hesitant to put down on paper the intimate details of my life. Irma coaxed, pleaded and reasoned with me about the necessity of doing it as the will of God. She offered many, many sacrifices that this mission for Christ might be accomplished.

In 1956, Jesus tested our confidence in a striking manner. One morning, after several days of internal bleeding, I collapsed in Irma's arms and was rushed to the hospital. They took X-rays to determine the location of the ulcer, and I was operated on at ten in the morning. The doctor told Irma he was amazed that I would not respond to any pain relievers or sedation. That night I began vomiting blood; at one the next morning, I was operated on again to check the bleeding. My physical suffering was bad enough, but was nothing compared to the spiritual torments that God allowed me to undergo. Again I was in that state where I seemed to have lost my faith, and the devil was allowed to trouble me severely. He said, "Is this the God you want to love? Is this the God you have tried to serve so faithfully? Look at what he is doing to you now!" I had to exert the greatest effort to keep from falling into despair. I didn't know if I had faith or any of the other virtues, but I wanted desperately to exercise them. That desire

was as far as I could get. Sometimes the only expression of faith, hope
or love that I could make was to press my lips to a little black crucifix
near my bed.

Before they put me to sleep for the second time in 24 hours, I
told the doctor, "Take good care of me; I have three little children
waiting for me at home." At that moment, the Blessed Mother of Christ
said to me, "Roy, what if Jesus wants to bring you to himself tonight?"
I said to our Blessed Mother with all the energy I could muster, "May
God's will be done!" As they were about to inject the anesthesia, I
whispered, "O my God, into your hands I commend my spirit." I did
this in blind trust and with a great pleading for the grace to love God
I was convinced that should I go to God that night, I would go as a
poor beggar.

I woke up about five in the morning with severe pains in my
stomach. I cried out, "Oh my God, oh my God!" I said to myself,
"I'm alive! Jesus and Mary must have been testing me!" Irma and I
shared the trials of a long period of convalescence. My spiritual darkness continued, and I was now deprived of attending Mass and receiving Christ in Holy Communion. I begged our Lord to come and unite
himself to my soul spiritually, but received no consolation. I found it
very hard to pray. Sometimes I couldn't even bring myself to speak the
words, "Thy will be done." Irma and the children were very sympathetic and tried to cheer me up, but their love and all the kindness
and affection of my relatives and friends comforted me very little.
I looked at an image of Christ on the cross and offered to him through
the hands of his Blessed Mother all the spiritual and physical torment
I was undergoing, without the knowledge that it was even acceptable
to him.

It was no help to know that some of the townspeople were saying,
"Look how God is punishing Roy." They convinced me that I was
getting what I really deserved. And added to all this torment was a
growing stack of unpaid bills.

25. A Bewildering Trial

Between Irma's wonderful care and the healthful spring weather, I finally recovered and returned to work in March of 1956. I had been under Father Frederick's spiritual direction for almost six years, but strangely, I found increasing difficulty in opening my heart to him. This pained me, for I couldn't say exactly what I was looking for from this wise and kind counselor. He was in failing health — I think he had had a mild stroke — and he was pressed for time, with many demands made upon him. Though Father Frederick's warm smile and patient understanding sustained my courage, I felt a need to seek another priest to guide me along the road to God. I asked the Holy Spirit to help me find another director if it was his will.

One night while at the Passionist Monastery, I saw a priest talking to a friend of mine. I knew nothing about this priest, yet I felt a powerful urge to speak to him. I approached him and introduced myself. I asked him to become my spiritual director and told him why. He refused. I begged him, but to no avail. He agreed to hear my confession and urged me to continue with my present director. I went home saddened and confused. I had never heard of anyone changing spiritual guides once God had led him to one. Again I feared that the devil was leading me into the trap of conceit, whereby I would tell every Tom, Dick and Harry of God's favors to me.

The next time Jesus made his presence felt, as he frequently did during this period to encourage me and increase my love for him, I told him he would have to direct me himself, as he had done in the past. Three days later, I received a telephone call from my friend, who had a message from this new priest I had met: he had changed his mind and would be happy to be my spiritual director. Surprised and pleased, I thanked our Lord for giving me the guide I had so painfully sought.

A few days later I went to the monastery and asked for Father. I told him I was grateful he had decided to help me along the mysterious path on which God had placed me, but that I felt like an ungrateful traitor leaving Father Frederick. He calmed my fears, assuring me that others had been known to change directors or to have several directors simultaneously. I told him all that God had done in lifting me from my misery, and how Christ had directed me personally for eight years. Father explained that no one came on his own to the path of spiritual perfection but had to be introduced into it by God. He felt that the graces I had received were not for myself alone; Christ was preparing me for some work which he would make known in his own good time. These graces, he insisted, were not strictly necessary for salvation; it was sufficient for a man to follow the ordinary means of grace in order to reach high states of sanctity. We talked about the teaching of Christ that all men are called to perfection.

He guided me with sympathetic firmness. I had no difficulty explaining my spiritual problems to him. I admired his great reverence toward the Holy Spirit, the ultimate Director of souls. He told me he was only acting as a guide, and he wanted me to follow the inspirations of the Holy Spirit. Whenever I had any specific problem I was to feel free to speak to him about it. I mentioned the idea of writing a book about my life and received his consent and encouragement. He calmed my fears, assuring me that the things which were happening to me on this path toward God were not figments of my imagination. In due time, under this wise man's direction, the strange events of my life and the whisperings of Christ in my soul began to form a clear pattern and make sense to me.

My new director measured my progress in the spiritual life by the observable effects in my everyday living. He told me that the graces God had given me were in harmony with my life as father of a family. I told him that sometimes, when people asked me to counsel them in their spiritual life, I hesitated to do so. He replied, "Roy, you have no right to refuse anyone whom God causes to cross your path asking for help. Whatever they confide in you, you bury in your heart and take it with you to your grave." Before embarking on any new apostolic activity, I always made my desires and plans known to him, knowing that his consent was an echo of God's will.

I often spent some time with Father Frederick talking about old times, and was sorry to see this wonderful man's health failing rapidly. On April 23, 1957, my director telephoned to say that Father Frederick had died suddenly from a stroke. My old fear of having betrayed him returned to add to my sorrow. The next day Irma and I took the children to pay him our final respects. We entered the chapel and walked down the aisle toward the simple black casket. As I knelt there with my family, I thanked God for having given me this great friend, the first priest in whom I had been able to confide. I knew that Father Frederick was now with God, who would let him see the reason why I had sought a new director.

After a time, I felt that Christ wanted me to communicate to others the message he had given me. My new director told me to feel free to do so. At the same time, he urged me to continue planning my book.

In September of 1957, Fidele, Syl, Mae and I set out for Canada in two cars to bring my brother Raymond, his wife and eight children to live in the States. This was the first opportunity in many years for all of my mother's children to gather around her. As we crossed the Canadian border, I began recalling many memories of my life in Canada, and in particular in Moncton, where Christ had first lifted me out of my misery. We enjoyed our family reunion for three wonderful days. The night before we were to leave, I gathered the family together and told them of the plans to write the story of my life. I wanted to give them an opportunity to speak up if they objected to revelations about our family life. I began to unfold to them my life with Christ since my illness and conversion. My stepfather was touched to hear how his statue of the Sacred Heart had been used by God in one of the early incidents of my spiritual life. When I finished, they all urged me to go ahead with my plans. Then my mother excused herself and left the room. I found her in the bedroom in tears. She told me she was overcome with gratitude to God. I put my arms around her and talked to her about the great goodness of God and the secrets Christ shared with me.

The next morning, my stepfather came to me with his statue of the Sacred Heart. He placed it in my hands and said, "I feel you should have this; in fact, I want you to have it. Pray for me and remember me." He started to cry as he reminisced about some of his failings in the years we had spent with him as youngsters. I assured him that God was understanding and that we all fail in many things. I said, "Pop, God is not going to forget the fact that you took in a bunch of homeless kids, and raised them as best you could. You suffered a lot, too, I remember." He kissed us all good-bye, and as he turned I heard him say to my sister, Beatrice, "I'll never see them again." He was then 75 years old.

In the fall of 1957, Irma and I settled in a larger home on King Street in Somersville; we were expecting another baby in January. Because of Irma's previous miscarriages, a gynecologist advised that she have her baby by Caesarian section. On January 26, 1958, I drove Irma to the maternity hospital in Springfield. The next morning at three o'clock, our doctor called to tell me he was preparing to operate and would like to have me there. I arrived at the hospital at 3:20 a.m., a minute after our boy was born. We named our new son Paul David, in honor of St. Paul of the Cross, founder of the Passionist Order, and David, ancient leader of the Jewish people.

I was working hard at two jobs — in the factory and at Scitico Market — trying to make ends meet. One day at the factory, Mary, the Mother of Jesus, stood beside me. She was dressed in white, with a blue sash around her waist, her hands joined in prayer. She made me understand that she was asking that Irma join me in praying and making sacrifices for the clergy. She also urged me to seek the prayers and sacrifices of many others for this same intention. She said she was aware of the suffering Irma and I were undergoing to preserve our marriage vows inviolate, and asked that we offer these sacrifices to win graces for the souls of priests.

To show me the urgency of her pleas, the Mother of God unfolded the awesome dignity of the priesthood, using various portions of Sacred Scripture to show me the nobility of their calling. She gave me a deep understanding of how Christ works through his priests to continue his ministry among the poor, the oppressed, the sick, the sinners and the dying, but that the spirit of worldliness was taking its toll among these chosen souls. She told me of a priest who was about to fall from his sacred calling because of the allurements of a woman. Several weeks later, the priest of whom she spoke, docked at New York and announced to reporters that he had just married this woman. This enlightening visitation from the Mother of Christ increased my reverence for priests. I knew that they had grave obligations before God for the salvation of souls and now realized that they were fighting against heavy odds not only to save the souls of others but their own.

I began to accept invitations to speak at Communion breakfasts, club meetings, etc., in order to speak of the love of God. It brought me great joy to stand before hundreds of men and women and pass on the wonderful message of God's love for us, which I had learned from Christ himself.

One of the finest examples of the cooperation that I wanted to see between priests and laity took place at a meeting of the Holy Name Society in a parish in Broad Brook, Connecticut. I was sitting in the front pew reading the Divine Office in preparation for Holy Mass when the pastor came to me on his way to the altar. He shook hands with me, welcomed me to his parish, encouraged me in my work, and told me he would pray that God would touch the hearts of his parishioners as I spoke to them. As he ascended the altar, our Blessed Lord made me realize that this priest and I, indeed all priests and laity, share in the royal priesthood of Christ, and must work together to bring the kingdom of Christ to perfect fulfillment in the world.

Introducing me to his congregation, he explained the nature and motivation of my work and asked them to pray that I might continue my efforts to draw men to Christ. After the Communion breakfast, Father introduced me to the Holy Name Society. He told them he had called my pastor to find out about me, because a pastor can't be too careful about who speaks to his people on spiritual matters. My pastor, he said, had trusted me enough to recommend me. My preaching throughout Connecticut was often tedious, but I was greatly helped by Irma's encouraging words. She realized that I had obligations beyond our family.

One day, my spiritual director told me that he no longer believed that my visionary experiences were from God. I told him that I wished I could agree with him, but if I did so I would be dishonest. I said I would have to die rather than deny that Christ had come to me and spoken to me. Still, his words dampened my spirits. I asked if he wanted me to burn my manuscript and he said, "No, put it away in your filing cabinet." He said he would continue to act as my confessor. Driving home to Somersville, I wondered why God had pulled this prop from under me. The devil called me an idiot for placing my trust in priests. I prayed to Christ to help me maintain peace of mind and soul. When I walked in the door at home, Irma shrieked, "What's happened to you?" I said, "Why?"

She cried, "Your face is white as a sheet!" I told her what had happened and she shook her head in bewilderment.

As I tossed and turned on my bed that night, I wondered what would become of me and my work for Christ. I got up around 2:30 a.m. to pray: "Dear God, what is going to happen to me? Have I been a victim of delusion all these years?" Satan again came to torment me. But then I heard an interior voice saying, "I live in you — you and I know the truth about the graces you have received and their effects upon you and others. I know that you love me, and I know of your sincerity. This incident which troubles you is allowed by me. You are now without all human support. You must of necessity throw yourself upon my care. Lean on me and be at peace." I was made to understand that I was again under the direct influence of the first Director of my soul — the Holy Spirit of God living in me.

I continued to see my spiritual father regularly, but every visit was painful, for I wanted him to believe and trust me. For two years, I avoided all mention of the graces I received from Christ. After confession we talked of things of mutual interest. I asked if he wanted me to discontinue my public speaking for Christ, but he encouraged me to keep up this work. There was no stiffness or coolness on the part of either of us; our conversation was often filled with humor, which helped to lighten my burden. Added to the cross of Father's disbelief was the pain of misunderstanding on the part of some of my friends; I felt drawn even closer to Christ, who had lost some of his followers and intimate companions. I found that I could not hope to please and win everyone even if I desired only to preach the ideals that Christ had preached. Jesus made me realize that the servant is not above his master.

One day, I said to my director, "If it's the devil who brought about my conversion to Christ, made me love God and my neighbor, taught me self-denial, and led me to practice the virtues of the married state — more power to him!" Father laughed. Later on, I told a friend, "If it's the devil who has thrown me into the arms of God and has made me struggle to keep his commandments and follow Christ with strong faith, hope and love — then God bless the devil!"

26. Christmas Joys in Our Town

There is in the hearts of all of us a special place for the birthdays of those who love us and whom we love. In my life, Jesus Christ has shown me more love than anyone and there is no one I love more than him. I cannot write the narrative of my life without relating an incident concerning the birthday of my Lord.

Ever since Christ lifted me from my misery and gave my life a purpose, the Christmas season had a saddening effect on me. Giving Christmas gifts is a wonderful expression of love for those near our hearts, but the fact is that in this great worldwide birthday party, the Guest of Honor is often neglected, and even forgotten. For a number of years, I prayed each Christmas that I might do something to bring Christ, the Lord of the world, to the attention of my fellowmen. I felt that if I could focus attention on Christ, they might come to understand the real meaning of his birth and perhaps give him their hearts in total commitment to his cause. I knew if this could be brought about, the cycle of gift-giving would no longer be one-sided, between man and man, but would find perfect fulfillment when men gave Christ what he most desires — the gift of themselves.

In December of 1952, I made a small beginning in my long-cherished plans to help put Christ back into Christmas. While getting my children ready for bed one night, I told them I had been thinking of a plan that would help them say "Happy Birthday" to Jesus in a very special manner. I put my arms around them and said, "Sharon, you are going to take the part of the Virgin Mary, and you can carry your doll as the Infant Christ. Roy will be St. Joseph, and Susan will be an angel. I'll play Christmas carols on my accordion, and one of Daddy's friends has agreed to play his mandolin."

Sharon and Roy spread the news around school, and I began to receive telephone calls from children wanting to join us. My sister Mae, who lived next door, helped me design cardboard wings for the angels, which we trimmed with Christmas tree tinsel. We made the angel costumes out of some bedsheets. Irma sewed a blue and white costume for Sharon, while I designed a heavy brown cloak for Roy. As the days passed, the children's excitement grew. I was happy to see this, for I felt that besides being a tribute to Christ, our efforts would teach my children one of the corporal works of mercy: we intended to reach as many invalids and elderly people as possible. I told the children, "A lot of these people would like to go to their churches on Christmas but, because of age and illness, they have to stay home. You are going to help brighten up the Christmas season for them."

Several of my co-workers in the mill asked if they could participate, and more schoolchildren knocked at my door to ask if they could sing with us. I couldn't outfit them all, so we contented ourselves with tying big red bows around their necks. When December 22 rolled around, we had 37 in our group. They assembled in our front yard in the bitter cold. We placed the children dressed in costumes at the head of the little procession, and then the other children and the adults followed. We played and sang "O Come All Ye Faithful" as we walked up School Street toward All Saints Church, where we gathered around the front door of the rectory. Although he was not feeling well, our pastor put on his hat and overcoat and came out on the porch to listen to us sing. He congratulated the children on how fine they looked and thanked all of us for coming to sing carols for him.

We toured the neighboring streets, and it was a delight to see the elderly peering through the windows, smiling and waving at the little children. In several homes, invalids were brought to the windows, and Sharon held up the Christ Child for them to see. As we reached the far end of Somersville, we circled the Congregational Church. We also stopped on the corner facing the mill and sang carols for those working the second shift. The sweetness of the mandolin blended with the music of my Irish accordion and the voices of the children and adults. I thought of how glorious that first Christmas night must have been with the angels singing, "Glory to God in the highest!"

When we arrived at our state senator's home, we sang carols as we filed into the front hall and then into the dining room, where his wife had arranged what was almost a banquet for us. She had bought ice-cream molds of Santa Claus, and the children laughed as they watched Santa melting away on their plates. I went to bed that night thanking God for having blessed our enterprise. We were told by many that our pageant was very meaningful to them.

In August of the following year, we made plans to form a larger group of carolers. We decided to have a float depicting the manger scene, with children playing the character roles. We contacted a local reporter, who wrote a stirring account of what we had done the previous year, and sent it to the *Springfield Daily News*. It gave us wonderful coverage. Our plans for the next Christmas were made known to millions through the press, radio and television. The Somersville Manufacturing Company gave us yards of fine red wool in which to dress the choir members, and a choice of colored cloth for the biblical scenes. We hoped to have one float, but received so many offers of cloth, money and helpers that we found we would have seven. Women formed sewing groups to make over 100 costumes for the choir — which was made up of Protestants, Catholics, and even some who had no church affiliation. Old enemies shook hands and worked with us, as men, women and children rallied around our group. I was the one who coordinated the various activities. We even had enough funds to buy a portable organ and amplifiers.

To obtain materials needed to dress the little girls as angels, a newspaper printed an article asking families to "adopt an angel" in the Christmas pageant. The hardworking people of this suburban New England town, 400 helpers in all, made many sacrifices to help realize my hopes.

A few days before Christmas, our gaily decorated group lined up near the mill for the first of many outings. When I gave the signal, the state trooper's car began its way up School Street, its red light flashing. The mill bell announced that we were on our way. The organ pealed out, and we sang our first carol, "Away in a Manger." The voices of men, women and children rang out in joyous song, telling of the birth of Jesus. Four thousand spectators had come to Somersville from surrounding towns and cities.

As we neared an area where the people were thickly congregated, Jesus appeared to me, telling me how pleased he was at the efforts we had all put into the celebration of his birth. He expressed his love for all of us and thanked me for persevering in this project. He knew I had been tempted to give up many times. The vision lasted for part of the Christmas tour. I was delighted to see the great throngs lining the streets, joining us in celebrating the feast of Christ's birth. It was very consoling to see so many families grouped together as we passed through each section of Somersville. The parked cars were filled with little children, pressing their noses against the windows so they wouldn't miss anything. The minister of the Congregational church greeted us warmly on the steps of his church, as did our pastor. I asked Jesus to fill the hearts of all with his love as our group moved slowly through the town in the stillness of the night.

The days that followed were filled with messages of good will, congratulations and gratitude. I was very proud of our town. In the following years we traveled with our pageant to many cities and towns. We were gratified to see many civic and religious organizations work so hard to help us, and to hear the church bells in these places rung simultaneously to announce the arrival of our Christmas pageant.

One year the pageant was almost ruined by a few people who tried to set our workers at odds. Some from each respective faith condemned us for working together as Catholics and Protestants, trying to arouse suspicions of insincerity and of a secret intention on the part of each religious group to try to convert the other.

A few days before we were to appear in Springfield, I was convinced that Satan had succeeded in tearing our project to shreds; I could see no way to unite the dissenting factions in our large group. Kneeling at the Communion rail in St. Bernard's Church in Hazardville, I saw Christ standing on the gospel side of the altar, dressed in white. He came down toward me and said, "Roy, the pageant will be a success; do not be afraid." I took courage from this and somehow was able to rekindle the original spirit that had driven us on in our work. I was overwhelmed at the crowd waiting for us in Springfield as our "living Christmas carol" wended its way through the majestic natural setting of Forest Park. The police estimated the crowd at well beyond 20,000.

Our committee accepted an invitation to appear on television with some of the characters and part of the choir. When asked why I put on the pageant, I simply spoke of Christ's love for everyone. Later, they told me my message was reaching millions. This brought me great joy, as I remembered many times that Jesus had pleaded with me to speak of his love for mankind.

27. My Altar of Sacrifice

In the spring of 1958, Irma and I were faced with a very grave decision. For several months Sharon had been pestering us to let her enter the convent after the eighth grade. Because of her youth we didn't place too much stock in her ambitions; but as time passed, she was more and more outspoken in her desire to serve Christ as a sister. She often talked with me for hours of her love for God and her desire to help others get to heaven. I explained all the aspects of such a vocation and urged her to pray for light. She increased her devotional practices and went about the house working in the spirit of a true religious. I was a little concerned, for I wanted her to enjoy a well-rounded, normal adolescence. We increased her sex instructions to give her a wholesome education in all the facets of young womanhood and to help her appreciate the joys of motherhood. I told her, "Sharon, you are not old enough to enter the convent. You will only be 14 in December." She said, "Oh, no, Daddy, I don't have to wait until I'm 18; there's a religious order in Boston that takes girls 13 years old." She showed me a circular from the Daughters of St. Paul, whose novitiate was in Jamaica Plain, Boston.

I told her she could write for information. I wrote to the superior, telling her my daughter was writing with my consent, and that I would appreciate any kindness extended to her. Within a week we received a gracious reply. They encouraged Sharon to keep up her daily practices of religion and to ask God's help in determining her choice of a state in life, and invited us to visit their novitiate.

On June 29, we drove to St. Paul's Convent to witness the investiture of several young postulants. The singing made the convent seem like a "little bit of heaven." After the ceremony, Mother Provincial spent some time questioning Sharon. She seemed content with her motivation in seeking admission to the St. Paul apostolate, that of the mass media — radio, television, printing and films. She calmed our fears concerning her youth, telling us that 13 was a good age to start out in the service of God. Sharon could enroll as a postulant and begin her high school studies in their junior scholastic program, which was affiliated with the Catholic University of America. She told us Sharon was acceptable to her, and needed only the required documents and a recommendation from our pastor. We asked for more time to think things over, as we wanted to be sure that letting our little girl leave our family so young would be in her best interests. We had never heard of a religious order accepting candidates at such an early age and were very skeptical; yet, we did not want to be an obstacle to the designs of God.

I took Sharon to see our pastor, and she told him how she wanted to give her whole life to God and serve others because of him. He said he could see no harm in letting her try convent life during high school. Still not convinced, I took her to see my spiritual director. He also urged us not to resist the graces which he felt God was giving to Sharon. I went home to think, unable to hide my sorrow at the thought of losing Sharon. I sympathized with Irma as she cried out several times during the month of July, "Don't rush me, don't rush me; I have to think!"

Again and again, we debated the question of such an early vocation. Sharon's tears showed how fearful she was that we might defer our consent until she was 18. One day Irma asked her how she could leave us and her new baby brother, whom she loved so much. Sharon answered, "Mommy, it's easy to do something hard when you do it for God." Irma then asked her, "Wouldn't you like to get married someday and have children of your own?" Sharon said, "In serving God and others, I will have thousands of spiritual children." After much prayerful thought, we gave our consent. I have never seen a girl more excited than Sharon as she made plans for her big day. She chose August 15, the feast of the Assumption, to enter — not only because of her love for Mary, but because

Irma and I had been married in Assumption Cathedral in Moncton.

Some relatives and friends did not appreciate our decision. I was accused of being a religious fanatic, forcing our daughter into a convent. But not everyone reacted unfavorably to Sharon's vocation. Several friends helped prepare her dowry and trousseau. We gave Sharon a send-off party and many came to wish her well and offer tokens of affection.

Two nights before she left, as we recited the family rosary, I put my arm around Sharon and asked if she wanted to postpone her entrance. "It's your privilege, sweetheart," I said, trying to reassure her. "No, Daddy, I want to go; but I was just thinking how I'm going to miss you and Mommy and the kids. I'm going to miss praying with you like this in the evening." I told her she would always be united with us in the Mystical Body of Christ and especially in the sacrament of Holy Communion. Through my mind flashed the thought of Abraham sacrificing his son. Perhaps a father can be forgiven a little self-pity at such a time.

On the way to the convent in our old car, we sang the hymns we often used during our family prayers. I tried to make the family laugh, without much success. A thunderstorm broke as we neared the convent, and the nuns ran out to greet us with umbrellas. Before leaving us to get dressed in her black robes, Sharon knelt in front of a life-sized statue of Christ and I gave her my parental blessing. Mother Provincial talked quietly to Irma and me until Sharon returned in her black dress and long lace veil. Irma and I embraced her; then the sisters served us all a lunch to celebrate God's calling of our daughter. Sharon smiled happily as she waved good-bye to us through the window.

The weeks that followed were painful ones. It was hard to sit down for meals and see that empty chair. Irma and I were convinced that we had acted according to God's will, but this didn't make things any easier. Sharon's rule permitted her to receive one letter a week from her parents and she was allowed to write one to us. I did most of the writing and kept her abreast of family activities. Her superiors allowed me to continue the spiritual direction I had been giving her as her father.

28. Stamps of Approval

In December, my mother telephoned from Canada; my step-father had been rushed to the hospital, apparently dying of cancer. Beatrice came to the phone, and I urged her to make sure that Pop could speak to a priest and prepare himself for death. She resisted, not wanting to frighten him. It took some time to make her realize that we have to face the hard realities of life, and that it would be cruel to deprive my stepfather of the special graces and help he would receive from God through a priest. I told her to keep us informed and then hung up. During my evening prayer, I reminded Christ that he had promised to look after all my interests, and the eternal welfare of my stepfather was an interest of prime importance.

On the morning of December 17, I was awakened by a call from my mother; my stepfather had died in his sleep, a few hours after receiving the last rites. I told Beatrice that as many of us as possible would come to Canada immediately to help arrange for his burial. This pleased her very much, for there were no men in the family to see her and Mom through this ordeal. That afternoon, Fidele, Mae, Syl and I boarded a train for Moncton. When we went to the Cathedral rectory to arrange for the funeral, the priest asked, "How is it that none of you are his real children but have come so far to do all you can for this man?" I said, "We owe him at least this much," then I told him how Pop had taken us in when we were poverty-stricken. The Canadian Legion gave Pop a military funeral.

172

Mom said that having us with her as we laid him to rest gave her strength and courage to go on. When I arrived home, Irma told me that she and I had received a Christmas bonus of a full week's pay from the mill. As it was Christmas, we wanted the children to have a good time, in spite of Pop's death.

In February, 1959, the owners of the market where I worked part-time asked if I would work full-time on the meat counter. I gave a week's notice at the mill, and on March 1, began my full-time employment at the market.

During March, I received two invitations to speak: one was to a large gathering of the Knights of Columbus and the other to a group of Catholic Daughters of America. Suspecting that my pastor was fearful about my activities as a layman, I asked for a few days to decide. I went to see him and told him what I suspected. He admitted I was right: "I've been thinking it over, and I don't think the Bishop would take too kindly to the idea of you speaking on spiritual matters. We priests go to seminaries for years and take very special training for this type of work. I would advise you to lie low." I spoke to my spiritual director about this and told him again of my desire to spend my life bringing the message of God's love to as many souls as possible, in simple workingmen's language. He replied, "I want you to go home, put these thoughts on paper, and address it to your bishop. Let him take it from there."

I wrote to the Bishop of Norwich, Connecticut, telling him briefly of my background and my desire to speak to others about Christ and his relevance in their lives. I mentioned my 15 years of activity in public speaking and asked him to judge my fitness for this work. I enclosed a number of newspaper clippings describing some of my lectures and their effect upon my hearers. Three days later, I received a gracious reply from the Bishop, commending me on my work: "I would be pleased to have you continue your efforts to make our Lord and the Faith better known and loved, as long as you do it under proper supervision and guidance. In practice, this would mean working ordinarily through existing approved societies or organizations: Holy Name Society, Retreat League, etc., and under the guidance of your parish priest, or with his approval." The Bishop encouraged me to offer my services to the Diocesan Speakers' Bureau and imparted the blessings of God to my apostolic activity.

I took the letter to my pastor, who then gave me his blessing. "Roy, I know you will do a lot of good. Don't ever give up." He said he had heard of weekly meetings at my home of a large group of men, married and single, and asked what we did. I explained that, after reciting the rosary, I tried to help them know Christ in his sacramental presence and in their daily prayer life. If men try to know and love Christ in this manner, he will cease to be just an historical person to them and will become a living reality in their lives. I told him, "I've often had misgivings about these meetings; I would like to see a priest present." Reminding me of his ill health, he said, "You can start as many of these groups as you want in the parish. There is no need for a priest to be there."

One night a member of our lay apostolate group introduced me to a priest from the Montfort Fathers. He told me he had heard of our meetings, and that he had been searching for 20 years for just such a group. He asked if he could use our group as a nucleus for a Legion of Mary Praesidium, and I agreed. He met with us several times; then with the cooperation of the staff of St. Francis Hospital in Hartford, we founded the Mother of Divine Love Praesidium, with headquarters in a room given to us by the hospital. We carried on much-needed works in and around the hospital for several years. When we disbanded, each member of the group began a new praesidium.

I kept Sharon informed of our activities. When I visited her on February 21, 1960, she invited me to the chapel for Benediction. As the priest placed the Sacred Host back in the tabernacle, I heard the voice of Christ speaking to me, "Roy, my designs for you and for your book will be accomplished." This statement from the Divine Master left me more convinced than ever that I must continue my writing and my speaking apostolate.

On March 15, my spiritual director phoned. He spoke with great excitement: "Roy, I have found the man!" "What man, Father?" I asked. "I have been speaking to a priest about your whole story, and he is inclined to believe everything that has happened to you and is anxious to meet you." "But Father," I said, "I thought you didn't believe in them anymore." He answered, "I have reversed my thinking on the matter, Roy. I let myself be influenced by another priest who was too young and inexperienced in these matters. Please forgive me; I know I gave you a bad time. You must have suffered greatly in the past two years." I told him he was quite right, and we both laughed. Father said it was imperative to come to the monastery at once, as the priest was leaving that evening. When I arrived, Father introduced me to his friend, who motioned to a chair and said, "Relax now, Roy, and don't be afraid of anything anymore."

As I unfolded my story, I apologized for my lack of formal education, thinking perhaps I wasn't reaching him. He said, "God has given you the highest form of education there is, in the things that really count. I am convinced that Christ has been leading you personally and preparing you for a mission. I agree with Father that you are called to write a book and to speak for the cause of Christ. Do everything in your power to master the art of communication and leave the rest to God. You remind me somewhat of Jeremiah the prophet. He felt much like you do — wondering how he could possibly carry the message of God's love to others." He showed a deep understanding of my story. "As soon as you have written all of your story, I will do what I can to help you get this message to people." He looked at my outline and said he believed Divine Providence had written this book in my heart and in my life. As Father gave me his blessing, I felt a great burden lifted from my shoulders.

He suggested that I buy a tape recorder. "You've been talking to me for two hours and had no problem expressing yourself or making yourself understood. Use the recorder whenever you feel inspired to pass on to others what you are experiencing. This will help you get used to the idea of opening up your heart and mind for the benefit of others." After a time, I got used to the recorder Irma bought for me, though there were many times when Irma and my friends had to prod me to get on with the dictation of this book, reminding me that I had no right to withhold what God had given me to share with others. Eventually my director placed me under obedience to persevere in writing this book.

29. Struggles and Conquests -- Tears and Joy

In the early summer of 1960, young Roy asked our permission to enter a preparatory seminary. Irma and I were reluctant to grant it, for Sharon's departure was still fresh in our memory. After long consideration, however, we decided to let him give it a try. This decision was a little easier, for we knew he would be allowed to come home for the Christmas holidays and summer vacation. I spoke to him several times of the importance of using his talents and energies, that he might come to the integrity of manhood in Christ. I told him of the wonderful joys of body and spirit that go with fatherhood and of the great mastery of self which is needed in the priesthood as well as in the life of a married man.

Roy shared our reverence for the priesthood. We explained to him that it would take great courage to be a man after the mind of Christ, that he could choose no greater hero to admire and imitate. We took him to the seminary on Labor Day weekend and left him with our blessing.

A short time later, Irma told me that she was expecting another baby. This pregnancy had not been planned, and some of my friends ridiculed us for misplaced trust in the rhythm method. But our trust was in God, and we paid no attention to them. Another baby would increase our financial burdens, but we were confident that God would provide. The doctor who had delivered Paul told us that with the same medication and a Caesarian section, we could expect a healthy, normal baby. We hoped our new baby would be a girl, as Susan was beginning to show signs of wanting to enter the convent with her sister. She had an outgoing nature, and I told her, "I don't think you could stop talking long enough to keep the silence of the convent!" Roy wasn't happy at the seminary — he decided to leave at the end of the school year — and we feared Susan might be unhappy if she left home, only 14.

On April 7, Irma presented me with another son, whom we named Scott Michael. As we watched Susan caring for her little brother, we told her we didn't think she was called to be a nun, that she was the "mother type," and we kidded her about some of the boys at school. She said, "Sure, I like boys, but I like God better."

Sharon informed us that she was to receive the full habit of the Daughters of St. Paul at the end of June and would be known as a "little sister" until she was old enough to enter the novitiate. A busload of relatives and friends came with us to see Sharon enter the chapel in her bridal gown and veil and walk toward the altar to become a spouse of Christ. Cardinal Cushing presented her with her religious garb; she left the chapel and returned dressed in the habit of a nun. We had brought a large wedding cake, and all took part in the wedding feast to honor Sharon and her Divine Bridegroom.

Susan wanted to be measured then and there for her postulant's dress, but Irma and I resisted, wanting more time for her to think things over. Roy had come home the day before, telling us he was sure he no longer desired to study for the priesthood, though he realized that some of his problems at school were of his own making.

In July, Sharon was allowed to come home for two days, and we arranged to have a Mass sung in our parish church in thanksgiving for her vocation. A Passionist priest came from Springfield to preach on vocations. Another Daughter of St. Paul came with Sharon and they set up a vocational exhibit in the basement of the church. We held a public reception for her, and many relatives, friends and parishioners came to wish her well. Susan pestered us to let her go to Boston with Sharon, but we prevailed on her to wait another year. She was interested in a young man, and I wanted her to settle any doubts in her own mind as to the path she would choose. She wondered why we were keeping her home when we had let Sharon go. I explained that they were two different persons and that there had never been any doubt in my mind about Sharon's vocation. "Susan, if you still want to go when the year is up, you can be sure you will get all the cooperation you want from us."

Meanwhile, in developing my apostolate, I felt that it was to be two-pronged in its objective. My main interest was in the souls of men; then I felt that anything I did to lead them to make a retreat and develop the God-life in them would make America the better for it. A country is only as good as the families of which it is composed. I have seen many spiritual transformations take place in houses of prayer, affecting entire families. The restoration of this basic unit of society is greatly helped by men who bring home from their retreat the radiant joy they have found in Christ.

The retreat movement in Enfield now has its own chapter, involving several parishes. Several pastors left their churches open around the clock on First Fridays, so that our men could rise from their beds at various hours of the night and kneel for an hour of prayer in the presence of the Blessed Sacrament. I believe it is because of these hours of prayer before Christ that the leaders of the retreat movement received the graces to touch the hearts of others. We went from town to town in all kinds of weather to speak to various organizations about the retreat work. While I spoke, another member would say the rosary to give me moral support.

One Sunday our new pastor stopped me at the church door. "Roy, would you teach Christian Doctrine to the CYO during the coming school term?" I asked, "How many students are there?" He told me that there would be around 175. "I will be there with you, but I would like you to do the talking." I thanked him for his confidence and promised I would help. In October, we began classes. I had never taught such a large group at one time. We met in the church basement, and I did the best I could to help these high school students know Christ as I had come to know him, stressing, of course, the gospels and the teachings of the Church. I used the same simple approach that I was using in private instructions in my home, and it seemed to go over well with them.

Some parents wanted me to return to the question-and-answer type of instruction that they had received 20 or 30 years before. But my aim was to teach about Christ in so convincing a manner that my hearers would accept him as the central reality of their lives; once they came to know Christ as he is, religion would mean more to them than parroting answers to questions. I tried to get other adults to help with the teaching program; some were willing, but didn't feel capable. The pastor established the Confraternity of Christian Doctrine in our parish, and we finally initiated a teachers' organization which we felt would benefit every child of the parish. Many times I felt like giving up this strenuous work, but Irma said to me, "I don't see how you can in good conscience reject this opportunity God has given you to help others. Someday the youngsters you are teaching will be grateful to you, and I'm sure God always will be."

I drew up a program to help these future mothers and fathers develop a life united to Christ. It was very discouraging to learn how little instruction and encouragement some of them were getting from their parents. But the majority of parents were grateful and very cooperative. I poured into these classes all that I had learned from Christ, and I spoke often of his love for them.

One night after class, a group of young men asked if I would give them sex instructions. "None of us are getting instructions, and we have never received any from our parents. We don't know the first thing about the real meaning of life and love." Father suggested we might get a doctor to come in and talk to the boys and girls separately. Nothing came of this idea, but we did buy several books which were meant to prepare adolescents to assume their place in the world. I did what I could to draw these children to the sacramental presence of Christ. I told them that in Christ living in their midst, they would find what they needed to live with joyful purpose. I went to several homes in town, asking invalids and elderly people to pray for this group of youngsters, particularly on the nights we gathered for instructions.

During all this time, my mother remained in Canada. I had kept her informed of our family activities and my apostolate. At long last, on March 17, 1962, I welcomed her, Beatrice and Dorothy to the United States as permanent residents. God had answered my prayers and brought our family together once again. They moved next door to us, and we spent many hours together talking over old times. Whenever anything appeared in the papers about my activities, my aging mother cut out the articles and pinned them on the dining room wall. She spent much time looking at them and showing them to her friends. I never forgot the terrible price she had paid to keep me with her when I was very young, and I thanked God for giving her the joy of seeing me working for his cause.

In July of that year, Irma and I bought a small ranch house in Somers, Connecticut, not far from where we were living. We took Susan, who had now finished her freshman year, to visit the house, hoping that when she saw it she would wait until graduating from high school to become a nun; we did need her help at home with the smaller ones. My wife and I realized now that both of us would have to continue working to provide a decent home for our family. Susan walked into the house and said, "Well, if I decide not to go into the convent, this wouldn't be hard to take. But you can be sure I won't be living here!" Young Roy was very pleased with the house and found a part-time job to help us keep the home we waited for so long.

Susan continued her plea to enter the convent and we finally consented. We took her for an interview with Mother Provincial and told her, "We will let her come to you, and, if you can help her control her talking, you will probably be very happy with her." She answered that in their particular work, a person who likes to talk could be a great asset. I explained I couldn't provide a dowry or even a trousseau for Susan. "We never refuse entrance to any girl who has the right motivation and the blessing of her parents," she replied. "We will see that Susan has everything she needs." She chose to enter on August 12, the feast of St. Clare, who, guided by St. Francis of Assisi, founded the Franciscan order of nuns. Susan said, "Daddy, I chose this date because of what the Third Order of St. Francis has done for you and for our family."

The day Susan entered the convent was a big one for all the nuns, who relished seeing one of their members welcome her own sister. She was no stranger to them, as she had been visiting them with us ever since Sharon's entrance, and she had spent a week working there to see if she would like convent life. It was a long, sad trip home with our three boys, who felt, as we did, that our girls were gone for good. However, before her profession Susan would find that God was calling her to another path. She is now a wife and mother.

In the fall of 1962, our parish acquired the old Keeney mansion on Main Street in Somersville, to be used for a future convent. In this building we had plenty of space to teach Christian Doctrine to our individual classes. I was assigned to the seniors. By then, we had our permanent pastor, who has been a source of inspiration and encouragement to me in my efforts to spread the kingdom of God. With Susan gone, we arranged for a baby-sitter once a week to watch the little boys while I taught. In August of 1963, we moved into our new home.

Roy graduated from high school in June of the next year. At the end of that month, he came with us to see Susan become a bride of Christ. We brought her a wedding cake, as we had done for Sharon. The nuns prepared a dinner in their refectory for the new sister and her family. On a Tuesday morning, we returned to the convent to see Sharon pronounce her first vows. Irma and I were greatly moved when we heard the Bishop say, "Sister Sharon, henceforth you shall be known as Sister Mary Irma."

In the fall, Roy enlisted in the United States Navy for four years. We had only our two little boys, doing their best to keep us young.

30. A Summary and a Preview

This is May 7, 1965. I have been on a leave of absence from my work in the supermarket since early March to revise my book. I hope to have it finished soon. It has cost me a great deal in labor and sweat, for I am not a writer. The only reason I even dared to begin this task is that our Lord told me to do it. I hope that the message which my life story tells will be received in the spirit in which it is written and that it might help many readers to find some new ray of hope — and that my stupidity has not gotten in the way of God's purpose in having me write. Tomorrow morning, from four to five, I am going to spend an hour in adoration before Christ in his sacramental presence. I will ask him again for all the graces I will need to present this book and to keep my trust in him whatever may follow.

In this last chapter, I would like to recall one incident which I feel was a foretaste of what will be the last moment of my life in this world. And, in a way, it seems to sum up much of what I have been trying to say in the previous chapters.

Christians, in their public worship of God, recite the ancient Creed, a prayer which says in part, "We believe in one Lord, Jesus Christ, the only-begotten Son of God, born of the Father before all ages; God of God, light of light, true God of true God." The truths contained in these words were forcibly impressed upon my mind by an experience which took place on a hot summer day in 1956.

182

I had left the mill with my clothing drenched in perspiration. My face and hands were dirty with grease and specks of wool. I went straight home, only a short walk from the mill gate. The house was empty. Irma was working the second shift, from 3:00 to 11:00 p.m., and the children were outside playing. As I entered the house, an unusual sense of fatigue came over me, and I did not even wash or change my clothes. I felt an urgent need to pray. The spiritual and physical sufferings which came from my feeling of abandonment by God had become very intense of late. Yet, I could not muster enough strength to recite the Divine Office which I customarily said after work, in keeping with the rule of the Third Order of St. Francis. This liturgical prayer usually took me about an hour. While many of the psalms and verses were comforting, there were also many of them which only increased my painful longing to see and be with Jesus.

Fearing the pain of spiritual hunger that the reading of the office might again cause me, I sat in a chair just inside the living room door and started to recite some other prayers which a Third Order Franciscan may say in place of the office. At this time in my life, however, it happened that almost every time I set my mind to pray, a sense of disgust would repel me. Yet the Third Order rule asked that I say these prayers daily, so I struggled through them. While I was doing this, a strange feeling came over me — as though I had been drugged. All my senses became numb, and I began slipping into a deep sleep. As my senses became deadened, I began to worry about my children, whom I could still hear playing outside the window. I was anxious for them not to come into the house without an adult being with them, for I was sure I was dying, and I didn't want them to find me dead. The thought of death didn't frighten me, for I felt a great love for God burning in my heart.

What made me so sure I was dying was that my soul seemed to be wrenched from my body and pulled with a frightening speed toward a blazing light, which I was seeing with my mind rather than with my eyes. It was a blinding radiance, seemingly without measure or dimension, spinning at an amazing speed in a clockwise motion. It had the force of a gigantic magnet and pulled me toward its center with incredible speed. There was an atmosphere of infinity about this luminous force for, as fast as I traveled toward its center I knew I could never reach it. It had a beautiful whiteness, which could only be, I thought, of God. The force toward which I was moving was infinitely superior to any force existing in nature.

I was aware that this was a purely spiritual experience. While my soul sped toward the light, my body was like a statue carved out of marble, cold, unfeeling, motionless in the chair. Even though the total newness of this experience frightened me, my soul wanted only to move toward the center of this great light. There is no power on earth to which I can compare the immensity of power emanating from this glorious light. Even the incredible swiftness of a space capsule winging its way through the outer reaches of space cannot begin to compare with the speed with which my soul traveled toward that awesome force. After traveling for what seemed to be a thousand years or more, the circular blazing light parted in the center. Through the opening, I saw Jesus Christ, the Son of God, coming toward me. He held out both arms to me in a wonderfully warm gesture of love. He seemed just as eager to welcome me as I was to go to him. I cried out, "O my Jesus!" and he opened his arms to receive me. I rested my head upon his breast and, as I did so, I became one with him in an embrace of love and perfect contentment. My soul became submerged in him, so to speak, and he drew me into the depths of this glorious light.

I became aware that I was united through him to God the Father and God the Holy Spirit. My *whole being* was caught up in a fusion of love. This experience was one of *total mutual surrender* of these three divine Persons in me and me in them. This experience defies all description. I was given to understand the title of Jesus, "the only-begotten Son of God." I felt that Jesus had united me inseparably to himself, and through him to the Blessed Trinity, in the bond of eternal love. It seemed to me that Jesus wanted this embrace of love and its effects to be for the most part his secret and mine. Since this is an experience which I cannot find human knowledge or words to fully share with my readers, it will, in a sense, always remain my secret. I can only babble incoherently if I try to tell you what passed between Jesus and myself.

I do not know how long this experience lasted or how I came to my senses. The first thing I remember was that I was standing in the kitchen greatly saddened that I was still part of this life. In comparison with what I had seen, this world seemed more than ever a lonely exile from my heavenly home. I later discussed all of this with my spiritual director and told him that the closest I could come to explaining my reaction to the divine embrace was to weakly compare it with the ravishing pleasure and ecstatic joy which come to man and wife surrendering themselves to each other in the embrace of their human love. I began to understand what Jesus had meant in the earlier years of my conversion when he used the

sacrament of marriage as a symbol of what he wanted to accomplish in me. In this wonderful spiritual embrace, he gave me a
delight and comfort which can never be explained this side of
heaven. He imparted to my lonely soul a lasting sense of his
presence within me, a presence which gives me deep peace of mind
and heart. Our Lord removed all the heartache which I had suffered
because of my longing for him, a yearning which had almost killed
me with grief. I thought of his words in the bible, that in heaven he
will remove all the wounds life has inflicted, and dry all tears.

It is true that I now see him only through a veil, as it were,
because I am still bound on earth. But I still do see him. This new
way of looking at God, quietly and lovingly in my soul, is far
superior to the manner in which Jesus walked and talked with me in
previous years. He had used these mysterious visits to instruct me
how to love God, and how this love must overflow in the service of
my brothers and sisters in the family of God. He gradually weaned
me away from the use of the senses and taught me to walk before
him "in spirit and in truth."

Because I am human, I now suffer greatly from the absence
of his many consoling visits. However, our relationship with God
is so far superior to anything within our human powers that we must
learn to walk before him by the power of his presence within us, in
perfect faith. This vision by faith is the new sight that Christ spoke
of when he said to his apostles at the Last Supper: "I will not
leave you orphans; I will come to you. Yet a little while and the
world no longer sees me. But you see me, for I live and you shall
live. In that day you will know that I am in the Father, and you
in me, and I in you." This ability to see our God through prayer
and love is given to us by the Holy Spirit who hovers over our life
and dwells in us. He alone can dispose us to feel at home in his
presence, here on earth, as we make our journey to that place
beyond the grave where we will gaze upon the eternal splendor of
our God and be caught up totally in his love. There, our faith and
hope will no longer be needed. We will see in full vision what
we have believed and what we now see only in a dark manner. We
will possess what we have so long hoped for. Love alone will remain,
for it is love which seals our everlasting union with God.

. . . I have been speaking of some of the personal experiences
of my life and of the wonderful way God has dealt with me. There
is no implication here that the pattern of my journey to God is
meant to be followed by anyone else. The Holy Spirit is the Guide of
souls, and leads each person individually, often along quite different

roads. He is the master of his own riches, and knows what is best for each. He can go wherever he wills and give to whomever he wills. If he has given to me so abundantly, it is only because of the generosity of his love, poured into the vast emptiness of my life. The important thing to know is that God *does* want to give the riches of his love to each one of his children. He wants to lead all to himself, along the path of childlike, trusting faith, strong hope, and burning love.

I had hoped, after my conversion, to walk toward God along the way of simple faith, but the Master's thoughts and ways were different from my own. I won't know until eternity why he called me to a strangely different path. But even along this path, I have had to rely totally and blindly on the Holy Spirit, who alone teaches, rules and sanctifies souls. There are many people I know who live Christlike lives and are very pleasing to God. They tell me that they have never experienced any sort of mystical visit from Christ, and yet I am sure that they "see" God as they live each day for him. They look at him with the very simple, direct vision of faith. This looking at God while we are still in the darkness of our exile rejoices and strengthens our heart, so that we can bear manfully all the burdens of our human condition.

The vision of faith also makes us want to walk before God in great humility, lest we abuse our free will and give up our rich inheritance in exchange for some trivial pleasures of earth. One cannot gaze upon him without loving him.

Many of us suffer from a lack of direction here on earth, because we have somehow failed to know Jesus Christ with a deep, personal knowledge. He has made himself available to men in every generation, promising that he would be with us until the end of the world. I have often wondered why there was so much indifference toward our wonderful Friend and Savior and why so many never seem to find him, even though he is so ready to reveal himself to them. Perhaps the answer is that we have not really looked for him. Perhaps we fear that in finding him we cannot go on loving ourselves. If we seek him with an upright heart and a sincere desire, we will be sure to find him.

To those who would like to find Christ, I can only say: try keeping his commandments, and he will manifest himself to you at once through the peace and joy you will experience. Search for him in the scriptures, and you will hear him speaking to you within the silent depths of your soul. Open your mind to him to learn his truth, and he will flood your spirit with the Light of Light. Open your heart to him through obedience and resignation to his will, and he will clasp you to his heart in the embrace of love. Trust him in everything that happens to you, and he will pour into your soul the sweetness of his love. Speak to him in urgent prayer. Read and study the psalms. Beg him in the words of the psalmist: "Create a clean heart in me, O Lord." Make this your plea for a complete conversion of life, freed from those things which are keeping you from living as a true child of God.

God wants us to enjoy the light of his love even in this world, and we can have this enjoyment, if only we are willing to let him enter into our life. If we refuse to allow Christ to purify our spirit through his action within us, we can never hope to be able to rest our eyes on the face of God, either here or hereafter. He wants us to prove ourselves now, during this present time of trial, so that we might spend eternity caught up in his eternal love. For this we were created — union with almighty God!

If we cooperate with Christ to the point that we become one in spirit with him and we are no longer our own but entirely his, then God the Father can look upon us and say, "Here are my other sons, in whom I am well pleased." He sent his Son into the world to enlighten it, and Jesus said of himself, "I am the light of the world." If we become united to him through living a virtuous life, he will be our light, too. Jesus has commanded us to let this light shine from within us before all men, that they may see our good works and glorify our Father in heaven. It is true that humility will always know a certain reserve, but love knows the time and place to speak and act. Jesus doesn't want us to hide this light under a bushel, for he is eager that all come to the knowledge of the truth. He knows that the truth we reveal to others will make men free. No matter where we might find ourselves — in prison cells, behind the Iron Curtain, or locked in the cell of our own ego — if we let our spirit soar above our human nature and our human limitations to the most high God who is always present to us, then we will be truly free, and no man can restrict or destroy our freedom. If anyone should crucify our flesh or pain our heart, he only increases our likeness to our crucified Lord and unites us more closely to him. If anyone should snuff the life from our body, then he has freed us forever, to rest in the bosom of our loving God.

The love of God which has been given to us cannot be kept locked up in our hearts; it must spread itself to others, touch other hearts, like the tiny flame of a match which ignites a long row of candles on the altar. I long to spread the light of God's love. I long to draw all mankind to the joy of seeing God. I long to help men come to that wedding feast which Christ spoke of. He wants every soul to be wedded to the Blessed Trinity for all eternity in a glorious union of love. He speaks of the fulfillment of our life as a great wedding feast with the God of love. He said that if we do not come prepared for the wedding feast, that is, if we do not have on the wedding garment of sanctifying grace, we will be cast out into the darkness, where there will be no joy, no love, but only weeping and endless regret.

It is because I want to see God's appeal for love answered by all mankind that I have undergone the pain of writing this book. I hope that our Lord will use it to help crowd the wedding hall. I hope to continue to do everything in my power to spread the invitations to the wedding feast, couched in the message of God's tender love for man. Men are ready for such a message. Their overburdened spirits need something substantial, and that is God.

I place this simple writing in the hands of the Lord Jesus Christ, and I beg him, out of the love he bears for his heavenly Father, to attach his powerful graces to every word I have written. Without the help of that blessed grace, the lines I have put down for my brothers and sisters under God will never bear fruit. God knows how much I have grown to love my fellowman because of my dear Lord Jesus. The new manner in which he has led me to look upon the veiled face of my Father in heaven makes me yearn for his eternal company. It is not easy to stay here in this exile. Yet, if by my presence here in the midst of God's family I can help to draw souls to our Father, I will gladly endure the pain of exile.

I beg him to give the world an abundance of saintly bishops and priests to radiate the eternal light of God's love in their ministry and in their private lives. I pray constantly for fathers and mothers of families, that they may demonstrate to the world the compatibility of Christian holiness with their vocation, for their marital love can reach its full flowering only when it is caught up in the tremendous love of God. I pray for all souls everywhere, and I suffer greatly at seeing God so little loved. It pains me to see the coldness and indifference of people all around me. Our Christian life has become so academic, so mechanical; there is need to spread anew the fire of divine Love. It must awaken all men to the real purpose of their existence. It must give them a new reason to want to live a new kind of life.

My own life — like the lives of so many — began on a note of tragedy. I was surely caught up in a web of hopelessness and uselessness, from which there was no human deliverance. But the goodness of God reached down to rescue me and to raise me up to the high level of Christian living. To walk the long, steep road along which God guided my steps, I have had to endure much physical and spiritual suffering. Yet, looking back on it all, I am filled only with gratitude to the loving God who has done so much for me. If I have responded to his invitations, it is only because of his grace, which overcame my inner weaknesses and rebelliousness, and drew me to himself.

I pray that you who read this book may have abundant graces from God; that your life, which may perhaps also be a journey from tragedy, will come to the final triumph of union with God in the eternal embrace of his love. And if, while reading this story of my life, you are tempted to think highly of me or wish that you could see what I have seen, I would leave you with this last thought: because Roy has seen, Roy has believed; blessed are they who have not seen, and yet believe.

Epilogue

Completing this book in 1965, the author was uncertain whether his last chapter would be the last chapter of his life. The Christ he came to know and love so well saw to it by a new and definite type of intervention within the Church that the entire story told herein was but the first chapter of a lifetime of service and dedication to God and his people.

The Second Vatican Council has made it unmistakably clear that every layman has a definite and unique role to play in the mission of the Church. It has emphasized the importance of our adoption as sons of God, the priesthood of the laity, and our co-responsibility with the clergy for the well-being of God's people. In essence, this is the exact same message which Christ taught this man by a different means.

The importance of this story does not lie in the mystical experiences granted to the author, but in the fact that Christ taught someone who thought that no one loved or needed him that he is an important, loved and gifted son of God with a responsibility to God and his people. This is, in fact, the essential teaching of the Council's decree on the laity: the laity are commissioned to the apostolate by the Lord himself.

In 1968, acting in a spirit of obedience to the Council (and not to private revelations), the author founded the Apostolic Formation

Center for Christian Renew-all, Incorporated. This Center is dedicated to bringing glory to God and peace to all men of good will by helping them to realize their importance and responsibilities in the sight of God. The work is based on fidelity and obedience to the Christ of the gospels and the teachings of his Church. Mr. Legere is now engaged full-time in counseling, writing and speaking for the cause of Christ. The Center sponsors weekends of apostolic formation for both men and women, days of recollection, and several local chapters of dedicated persons of good will, who meet weekly for prayer, reading of the scriptures, and mutual help in following Christ. The formation these people receive stabilizes them in obedience to the commandments of God, the yardstick of our love for him, and has helped literally thousands to renew themselves and their families according to the mind of Christ.

The years of preparation recounted in this book are bearing fruit because this man preaches Christ and him crucified — not Christ and the visionary. His efforts for the Church have brought him the consoling personal encouragement of Pope Paul VI and several bishops. The development of this apostolate is a perfect illustration of the teaching of the Council that extraordinary charisms from God are only fruitful within the framework of obedience to authority. Response to these charisms, coupled with obedience, has made this man a dynamic apostle of the Lord for the building up of all mankind in Christ.

What God has done in a special way for this man, the Council reminds us, he is willing to do in an equally unique and personal way for everyone. This book should not lead one to expect or seek mystical experiences, but to recognize the advances of Christ in the ordinary circumstances, the wordless communications, of ordinary life. This man is but one of God's sons. The value of his message to the world is in the timeless words of scripture: "I will be your God and you will be my people!"

—Donald J. Philip